This, That and Some Other Kingdom Stories

Danny Martin West

Mossy Creek **PRESS**
CARSON-NEWMAN COLLEGE

This, That and Some Other Kingdom Stories

Danny Martin West

Mossy Creek Press
121 Holly Trail NW
Cleveland, TN 37311

This book was printed in the United States of America.

To order additional copies of this book, contact:

Mossy Creek Press
1-423-475-7308
www.mossycreekpress.com

Dedication

For my beloved family:

Merton and Fanny West, nurturers of my past;

Jeanne, Tara, Megan, Cameron, Jordan and Sarah,
sustainers of my present;

and my hope for the future, precious Matilda."

Table of Contents

Preface

IN 1995, WHILE LIVING IN KINGSPORT, Tennessee, I was contacted by Becky Whitlock inquiring if I might be interested in writing a regular religious column for the *Kingsport Times News*. Becky is an editor for the paper and had evidently come across some of my writings from my local church newsletter. I agreed to do so and have enjoyed a wonderful relationship with the paper and the larger East Tennessee community ever since. There have been seasons in which I have taken an editorial "breather" but, for the most part, I have been writing regularly since that time.

One of the things I determined early on in my writing for the paper is that I would predominately write about things of which I was familiar and that was the life and ministry of the church. I have doggedly avoided partisan politics, both religious and secular, through the years and I have attempted, at least, to be an encouraging voice for those whom I served through the print media.

I have not avoided subjects per se, but I neither did I set out for my column to be a bully pulpit or a flashpoint. I was not always successful, of course. I have been utterly amazed at the response my observations have generated. At times I felt like Glenn Campbell's "Rhinestone Cowboy" getting "cards and letters from people I don't even know." I truly wish I had kept a journal of the overwhelmingly positive and kind things folks have said to me in reference to a particular column or theme. It has been a blessing to connect in this manner with interested friends. On occasion, I have been harshly reprimanded by someone who took offense at something I wrote. While that was never my intention, there were inevitable moments when, in the words of the old country preacher, "I must have plowed too close to the corn." I received my fair share of criticism but it was normally couched in helpful language (normally, not always!).

As a minister, one of the better gifts I enjoy is that I am an observer of life. I don't live life with my eyes and ears closed to the realities around me. It has been the fostering of that gift that has serviced me well in my service to the church. I am fully convinced that the best ministers are those who know how to intersect the human story with the God story; when I do that well, my preaching and teaching is at its best. I enjoy listening to the stories and reading the lives of those around me. Much of what is included in the following compilation is just that.

I am grateful to Dr. David Tullock who pushed me to initiate this project. We have been friends a long time and I am appreciative that our paths cross once more. Most importantly, I am indebted to my wife, Jeanne, my three wonderful children, Tara, Megan, and Cameron, my son-in-law Jordan, and daughter-in-law Sarah, and my spectacular granddaughter, Matilda. They, along with a host of friends, have urged me to "do something" with sixteen years of columns and now that time has come.

The Arms of Moses

THERE IS A POWERFUL IMAGE recorded in Exodus chapter seventeen. The children of Israel have wandered in the wilderness for forty years and they are tired. They are also feeling sorry for themselves. Thus they begin to complain to Moses, accusing him of plotting to kill them, their children and their livestock in the desert. They are demanding water. Moses takes their plight before the Lord and God orders Moses to take his rod and strike the rock at Horeb and water would come gushing out. The water came! Immediately, the story shifts to a battle between the Israelites and the Amalekites. Moses stood upon the hill overlooking the battle. When he raised his hands holding the rod, the battle went well. But when he wearied and lowered his arms, the battle turned. Aaron and Hur then intervened. They perched Moses upon a rock (like a stool upon which he could sit) and when his arms wearied, they stood one on each side of him to hold them up (Ex 17:17).

It is a strange and unusual thing for caregivers to provide ministry to their leader. Aaron and Hur did it. Many others have done it. Currently, I am observing a congregation do that very thing. A young minister in my community has a catastrophic illness that is within weeks of taking his life. He has served his church faithfully and with integrity. For the last six months, however, this hideous disease has quickly robbed him of his vitality and his ability to work.

The church was faced with a very difficult set of circumstances. Their pastor, though still alive, could no longer function. Unlike many churches of which I am aware, this church has chosen the high and redemptive road. I have in my file countless horror stories of churches who when facing similar circumstances merely said to the minister, "Sorry, preacher. We know this is tough for you but we are going to have to terminate you. We wish you well." That response is the response of the world. For the world says it is every man, woman, and child for themselves. The world simply doesn't care and sometimes worldly churches don't care either.

This church could have taken the easy road but the easy road is rarely the right road. They have chosen to pour themselves out on behalf of this poor minister and his family. They are meeting every financial need. They are providing every practical and imaginable service to the minister and his family. It is a stunning and rare example of what the church is supposed to do.

They are holding up the arms of Moses. They have chosen to surround their pastor with unflinching love and support. And as they surround him, they are doing for him what he cannot do for himself. They are holding up his arms. They are encouraging him. They are providing for him. They love him and they are praying for him. Frankly, what I see is a very rare thing indeed. It is the church of Jesus Christ living up to its calling.

I have reminded this beloved congregation that what they are doing defies the odds. Too few churches respond with this level of grace and compassion. Moreover, I am reminding them that everyone is watching them. The world is watching eager to see if "those Christians down at the church" are really who they say they are. Other churches are watching them. They, too, want to see what kind of fellowship it is. Even God is watching. Every move and every gesture does not go unnoticed by our God.

I am convinced that as God watches his children "hold up the arms" of their Moses, he is proud and honored. I can almost hear the whispers from heaven, "Well done, my good and faithful servants."

On Being Honest with the Bible

O NE OF THE MOST CURIOUS THINGS I encounter in my faith pertains to the differences we all possess in our interpretation of that faith. I especially run into this reality by virtue of the itinerant nature of my ministry. I frequently worship and serve in different congregations and I am utterly amazed at how churches that espouse sameness in the Christian faith are wildly different.

Perhaps the greatest area of divergence and dispute is found in matters of biblical interpretation. Isn't it interesting how two people can read the identical passage of scripture and come out on opposite sides of the text? And even more intriguing is that both are often adamant that his or her view is the only way and the way that God intended the text to be read. I used to think such disagreement was a tad humorous; I'm not so sure anymore for I've detected dangerous and radical spirits in the church today that are mean and vindictive against those with whom we disagree.

Recently I was conducting a Bible study in a church and we spend a good bit of time discussing a particular passage of scripture. In this particular conversation I noted that the dominant voice in the room (there is always one, isn't there?) was examining the text in very literal sense. I gently noted that his interpretation opened up some very troublesome doors if he insisted on following a purely literalistic approach. In the ensuing discussion, several in the room began to pick up on the narrowness of method our friend employed in his biblical inquiry. My purpose was simple: I wanted this fellow to own up to his literalism and then I wanted to force consistency upon him. His approach to Bible study involved selective literalism which I guess is fine. But who among us gets to choose which passages are strained and which ones get a free pass?

Most in the room got it. They recognized that if you force a passage into a particular mold it holds true that all passages must be addressed that way. A biblical interpreter cannot arbitrarily choose to make some passages literal to prove a point and then play fast and loose with other passages that don't conclude the way the individual desires.

That approach drives me nuts and is wholly disingenuous. Be honest with the biblical text. Don't allow personal opinion and prejudice to shadow the message and meaning. Where this issue is especially thorny is with hard headed biblical students who refuse to often see the truth of the passage—especially if that truth counters some tradition or prejudice.

I would hope that all of us would be mature and reasonable enough to tackle matters in the Bible with honesty and maturity. Seek the truth of the text and then let everything else we bring to that moment fall under its shadow and authority.

Biblically Illiterate

THE DECLINE IN BIBLICAL LITERACY IS AN ISSUE that the Christian church must quickly address. Many churches rely upon alternate sources of authority to inform their members and the resulting effect of spiritual decline quickly follows. Recent studies remind us that many Christian adults know very little about the content and story of the Bible. In fact many believe that common phrases and urban legends are the stuff of scripture.

In a recent conference I listened with amazement (and a tinge of sadness) as a delightful college freshman from prestigious Stanford University, shared the experiences of her youth in developing her spiritual formation. The young lady was from a very religious home and she was the president of her youth group. When she was sixteen, she was nominated and ultimately chosen to be a participant in a youth camp for emerging Christian teen leaders. This was the first time the young lady had shared in such an event of this nature.

On the first day of camp, she was asked to read a verse of scripture from Genesis. The girl opened her Bible to the first book of the Bible but from that point on she was completely lost. She did not know that the Bible was arranged with chapters and verses for easy reading. She simply knew about the book of Genesis. With the help of bewildered friend (after all this was a camp for religious leadership) the girl was able to find the appropriate passage. For the first time in her life this teenage girl held in her own hands and read with her own eyes the words of the Bible. She was not from an oppressive third world country; she was from Indiana.

When I heard her story I was stunned and saddened. This young lady had been a part of her church for sixteen years and knew absolutely nothing about the Bible. I could not help but notice her denominational affiliation and as I did I remembered how obscure the group is. From the scant evidence that I saw from this young lady, there is little doubt in my mind the group will eventually disappear like a mist. For if a Christian church does not even introduce their members to the text of holy scripture, there can be no doubt the group is in trouble.

I see this trend clearly exemplified in the lives of many adults in the church. Their inability to navigate scripture and understand its content is alarming. With the onslaught of "Christian" literature that permeates our culture, more and more believers rely upon the fanciful and sometimes heretical views of others for religious training instead of engaging the biblical text themselves.

Because of this biblical illiteracy, the preaching task has grown increasingly complex. As a preacher you can no longer assume that the listener in the pew knows what you are talking about. This is not only true for those who grew up outside of the church; it is also reflective of those raised under the steeple. As a result of this biblical ignorance, it is increasingly vital that preaching provide appropriate biblical story and narrative. Folks in the pews do not know the stories of the Bible.

It is never too late to open the ancient text and learn its story. Teach it to your sons and daughters. And for the generational gap that is present today, teach it to your grandsons and daughters. The word is too important to be relegated to the back shelves of our Sunday school classes and church curriculum. Its message is too insightful to not build your sermons upon it. The word spared through the centuries is a word we need to know.

Mr. Frank

W E CALLED HIM "MR. FRANK" (not his real name). He was my Sunday school teacher as a child growing up on the coastal waters of Virginia. Mr. Frank was a self-employed waterman in my hometown who made an honest living at his trade. He was a man known for his character and integrity. Mr. Frank was universally known as a saint. People sought his counsel and wisdom. The hurting and the confused went to him for solace and love. He was a good man.

I long admired this good man from a distance. He knew and loved the children of the church and generously supplied us with chewing gum and candy on Sunday mornings. But it was not until I promoted to the fifth grade Sunday school class that I truly came to know Mr. Frank. I had heard the wonderful stories about his class and his deep devotion to the boys under his care. I was so eager to become one of Mr. Frank's boys, a title held with a note of reverence in our church.

So you can imagine my deep disappointment at attending my first Sunday school class with Mr. Frank and discovering that most of the boys in the fifth grade class could read and communicate much better than our teacher. Mr. Frank labored to read simple Bible passages. He grossly mispronounced biblical names, places, and even books. I quickly discovered that this revered man was virtually illiterate! And here he was teaching fifth grade boys.

I can vividly recall the drive home from church after that first experience with Mr. Frank. Sitting in the back seat, leaning forward and resting my chin on the front seat, I told my parents about how wrong we all were about Mr. Frank. He wasn't a good teacher, he wasn't a good teacher at all—in fact, he could barely read. I jokingly recounted for them all of the mispronounced biblical books I had counted that morning.

My father stopped me and gave me a harsh reprimand about my lack of consideration for Mr. Frank. "Give him a chance," were the words my father kept repeating. I had no choice in the matter and finished out the year with the worst teacher in the history of the church. Mr. Frank kept us in stitches with his mispronunciations and grammatical mumble-jumble. And to be honest, I'm not sure I learned anything about the Bible that year. It wasn't until I advanced to the sixth-grade class that I discovered what was right in front of me all along.

Our sixth-grade teacher was very accomplished. She was polished, sophisticated, and names like Melchizedek and Jehoiakim rolled off her tongue with following dignity. But something was missing. She was cold and aloof. She didn't seem to enjoy the sixth-grade boys at all.

Never once did she call on Saturday night to encourage us to be in Sunday school as was Mr. Frank's practice. She didn't ask about our school work, little league baseball, or anything of value in the life of a little boy. All she did was teach the lesson and go home. I started to think that maybe Mr. Frank had something to offer after all.

When he died a few years ago, it dawned on my how influential this one simple man had been in my life. He kept in touch with me through college, seminary, and beyond. He was as proud as punch the day my home church ordained me to ministry.

Sadly, I never really understood all that this simple man could have taught me. I missed so much wisdom because I was looking in all the wrong places. In technical terms, he was a very poor teacher. But I have learned that those are not the most important measurements of a man or a woman. Mr. Frank taught me about the wonder of simple things, the joy of living, and wisdom of simply loving God and loving others.

In truth, this very "poor" teacher continues to lend his brand of wisdom to me everyday. What more could one ask of a teacher?

Oh, the Joys of Church League Basketball

I GUESS IT IS A MIRACLE THAT what I faced recently in service to the church hasn't happened before. I tread cautiously here for I know that I will anger and irk some folks and that is not my intention at all. It is merely an observation.

My most recent interim pastorate experienced a very shameful and embarrassing moment that occurred in the heat of the battle of a church league basketball game. When the news of what had happened reached my ears it was too late for action for the season was over. But what happened has tainted my thinking on the role that "church league" athletics plays in the kingdom.

A young man was "recruited" to play basketball for the church. Now let's be honest. The recruitment was purely selfish. He has a nice jump shot and he can leap like a kangaroo. To defend his "recruitment" the coach of the team employed exaggerated religious language that went something like this: "John (not his name) needs to be in church and basketball is the tool that God has given us. We will use it as an "outreach." There is lots of religious code in that defense but let me interpret it for those of you who are unknowing. "John is a great basketball player and we want to win the trophy this year. So we will force him to attend church once a month. We might see him after the season but the chances are slim. But at least we will have the trophy."

Well, in the next to the last game of the season, John argued an officials call. The official did not respond to John. He rightfully ignored him. But then John crossed the line. He started to berate the official using horrific and profane language. And in that language he employed vile racial slurs. The official on the receiving end of this tirade happens to be a minister in the community and he happens to be black.

I am told that his response was very calm and very swift. He blew the whistle and appropriately said, "This game is over." And it should have been!

Naturally, John has never returned to the church. Truth is, he never intended to.

Since that event I have attended several church league games at the local YMCA and I have done so in a purely objective manner. I don't know the churches and I don't know the players. I have gone to do "social research" by observation. Mind you I am no stranger to these leagues. I have played church league sports for almost twenty years and enjoyed it. But in all honesty I admit now what I would not admit then; there is a dark and seemly side to these events that must be addressed. As an outsider I have watched teams and churches in recent weeks and I am appalled at what has always been but what I frankly did not want to confront.

The behavior, the attitude, the profanity, the brutality is appalling. I already know that many will take offense at my observations and attempt to defend their churches and players. Good luck. I actually called a pastor of one of the churches (who happens to be a very close friend) and I asked him if he had watched his church team compete. Being a very busy man he admitted that he had not. I gently said, "Jim, you need to see the 'witness' your church is putting on the floor every night." I don't know if my friend has seen his church team play or not. But knowing him as I do he would not endorse the antics or the vocabulary that I have witnessed.

Somehow church leaders must resolve two issues: how do we use church sports to appropriately "recruit" persons to not only play the games but to be led to a meaningful relationship to God? And how do we incorporate often non-Christian persons onto our team who may help win a trophy but through their actions help the church forfeit something far greater?

I don't have the answers and I am not trying to be a curmudgeon. I simply think that church leaders need to be more attentive to this issue and to exercise greater accountability.

So. . . play ball. Have fun. I certainly do. But don't forget it is just a game and don't forget about the church and the Kingdom that are to be represented in the effort.

Too Friendly for Our Own Good

I AM ALWAYS INTRIGUED WITH CHURCH greeting times before worship. Some are done rather orderly and with no fanfare. Visitors are asked to raise their hands and a visitor's card is distributed. Others ask members to stand and the visitor's to remain seated. Neither way really appeals to me. The worst thing I have ever seen, however, is what I call the congregational free-for-all. That is when the whole church stops the service and roams the congregation seeking to greet others.

I have recently started with a church where the latter approach to greeting is the norm and the first time it happened it felt as if the whole service was out of control. The choir came down from the choir loft and roamed to the back of the sanctuary. Those in the back of the church made their way to the front. I have never seen anything quite like it. For almost ten minutes the worship service was "suspended" so we could greet one another.

All the while I am thinking, "Who is this service really for?" Is the service about God or is it about us? That is not the most troubling thing I observed. Those who were greeted were the mainstream members of the church. There were several visitors in attendance that day and I could not help but note that in the welcome time the visitors were almost entirely neglected while the familiar folks hugged and greeted one another.

There was one lady in particular that stood out. She was clearly a newcomer to the church and she stood in the corner of the back section by herself. She was not really by herself, mind you; there were folks all around hugging and shaking. But there she stood all alone.

I tried my best to get back to her to provide a welcome and it was virtually impossible to get to her for the chaos around us. I finally made it to her vicinity and welcomed her. But all the while I was thinking, "if I were this lady, I would never come back here again." The members of the church had time for themselves and no time for the visitor.

I know these people and that would never be their intention. In fact they would be upset to think that I think they were rude to a guest. But they were. It was unintentional but it happened nonetheless.

Churches are sometimes so friendly that they are unfriendly. I mean by that that we are so loving and welcoming to those we know, we tend to miss those we don't know. We are friendly to the familiar and in turn inhospitable to the stranger.

Most of the churches I know are very friendly but they are oblivious to the blind spots that often creep into our worship. One of these blind spots is the poor way we welcome guests. We either embarrass them publicly by singling them out with too much attention, or we humiliate them by offering too little attention.

We must find ways to appropriately welcome the stranger but not make them feel uncomfortable. The rule of thumb, I think, is to treat them as we would like to be treated. As for me, a warm personal greeting is far more effective than a full blown production in front of the whole church. But even more important is the necessity to greet the stranger and not leave them feeling left out. For if we do that we can be assured they will not come back.

The lady I mentioned has not returned. Some of the members are disappointed. I am too in a way but I am not surprised. Had I stood alone as she did, I would not have returned either. Think about it.

The Circle of Life

BACK IN AUGUST I USED THE WRITER of Ecclesiastes to serve as a launching point about the rhythm of life. Indeed the poet describes the ebb and flow of life perfectly: "To everything there is a season." I have long known about that truth. I have experienced it vocationally as God has moved me about the country with new opportunities of ministry and growth ever before me. I have encountered it in my personal life with the birth of my babies, the weddings of my children, and ultimately with the passing of my father. "To everything there is a season" is more than a beautiful sentiment it is truth and we all know it to be so. Some don't interpret the seasons very well. Some become bitter and cynical when the circle of life advances but advance it always does. Life follows death and death follows life. It is the way it has always been and that immutable truth will not change whether we like it or not. My advice is to own up to the seasons and enjoy them for what they offer. They can't be changed so receive them in joy knowing that each season lasts for but a moment in time.

Last week the circle of life moved definitively in my life with the arrival of a new baby in our family. Yours truly is pleased to announce for all of East Tennessee (heck, why stop with Tennessee? This news holds international significance) to hear that a spectacular little girl has joined our family. We prayed and waited, waited and prayed and on January 23 she made her grand appearance. She is beautiful, healthy, and extravagantly loved. Her coming has reminded me of the power of the circle of life—the seasons of life.

Actually, I've been quite low key about the whole matter. I don't intrude into conversations by opening up photo albums and I haven't bored folks to tears with our stories. While my wife and I are utterly thrilled and blessed by this experience, once the euphoria passed, I have found myself quite introspective. Like Mary of old, there has been some "pondering" time for me. I've thought a lot about my daughter, Tara, and how quickly she has grown into a beautiful young lady and now mother. The pride on her face and the glimmer of love in her eyes for her daughter is an image I will not soon forget.

I've thought about family members who are no longer with us and who would be giddy about this event. I have been surprised by the power of the emotions I have faced as I've remembered the dead even as I've basked in the glow of new life. In truth, there has been a wonderful reunion in my spirit in recent days. There the living and the dead have shared holy space together.

One of my students just asked me if this event has changed me. I could not lie, it has; it ought to, in fact. If the advancing of the circle doesn't cause one to reflect upon one's own life and journey, then that person is either oblivious or an idiot. I pray that I am neither. For me, at least, I have been drawing from a deep well in recent days. I am personally and forever changed by the presence of new life in my midst. She is, in part, from my flesh and blood. She has taken her rightful place in our family line and we are so blessed that she will join as a torchbearer of our legacy and story well into the next generation. Lord knows we needed someone to do it. The rest of us have been at this for a while now. We are weathered, tired, and a tad cynical about the things we see and the direction our world is headed.

That's why God shakes things up on occasion. He sends babies into the world to give us hope. Our prayer is that the little ones can straighten out the mess that the rest of us have made. God has always believed that babies can make a difference. It was his method in the sending of his own child centuries ago and it is still his method of choice these many years later. The circle of life continues. . . and we celebrate by giving thanks.

When Culture Trumps the Church

THE CHURCH IS ON A COLLISION course with culture and it appears to me that the church is going to lose! I recognize, of course, that Jesus said that the church would ultimately stand tall even against the "gates of hell." (Matthew 16). In the grand scheme of things, God and God's church will triumph. I am merely speaking of the here and now.

The church is not faring well in "head to head" competition with culture. For example: I grew up in a home where church took priority in our lives. I never woke up on Sunday morning and wondered if we were going to church that day or not. It was assumed and expected; we were going on Sunday morning, Sunday night, and Wednesday. If there were special services offered at other times, chances are we were in attendance for those, too. That kind of assumption is no longer in place.

I have noted a discernable and disturbing trend in recent years. Church is not as important as other institutions. For example, the church where I currently serve is blessed to have a bountiful number of young families. Let me rephrase that: the church has a bountiful number of young families but they are difficult to find. They live lives that run parallel to the church. They maintain a cordial relationship **to** the church but they aren't serious at all **about** the church. To that end I'm not sure the church is blessed at all. Most of these young families have children that participate in highly competitive athletic endeavors. As all of my friends know, I am a sports fanatic. I love sports! I always have and I always will. But I also made a promise to God that nothing would interfere with my relationship to him. Thus worship participation is a key for me. Not so with these families and so many more. Several have made it abundantly clear that baseball and soccer are more important than anything else in their child's development. Their children do not participate in sacred activities but they sure find the time to travel every weekend in pursuit of the secular. No doubt some will think I am but an old "fuddy duddy" and well I might be. But I also know that children in particular need spiritual guidance and grounding. That formational work will not and cannot occur when they are older. That work is vital in the process of family. Indeed in the biblical framework, teaching our children about God is our most pressing obligation. It is more important than teaching a young one to throw a curve ball or how to kick a soccer ball. That is important, too; but it is not critical.

The problem is really quite simple. Cultural values and priorities have supplanted Godly ideals in the lives of far too many. Every time a family or the church blinks to culture, one more Kingdom battle has been lost. Indeed, one of the offending parents once said to me, "These competitive leagues will only last a few more years, preacher and then my children will be in church." My response was swift and probably not as kind hearted as I would have liked but I said, "Yes, and they are very important years in the life of your child, aren't they?"

I am eager to see children participate in a wide range of activities; heaven knows that mine did. They played soccer, baseball, basketball, piano, violin, and they took dance lessons, too! But that is not all they did. My wife and I wanted there to be rightful balance in their lives. They needed God. They needed structure. They needed balance. So they were in church having the right foundations established in their lives. I fail to see that balance being offered very much anymore. I know it is still present in many wonderful homes and families; I also know that it is missing in far too many others. This is serious business and it is clearly something we have to think about.

Coins in the Communion Cup

IT IS ONE OF THOSE MEMORIES THAT I will never be able to erase. He was 82 years old and it was allegedly his first time in church. He sat in my vicinity and made a lot of noise in the worship service. Later I discovered that he was quite hard of hearing so his whispered questions were in fact shouts. He didn't understand anything that was happening that day. He looked around, talked a lot, and was quite distracting. But he must have enjoyed himself because he was in attendance the next Sunday.

What happened that Sunday still brings me to tears of laughter. Have you ever revisited a memory and for just a moment you can feel, hear, and smell everything that surrounded the event? That is happening to me even as I write. I am a 10-year-old boy all over again. The Sunday morning service was devoted to the observance of the Lord's Supper as we call it in Baptist life. It was an ordinary day with ordinary expectations. And then it happened. When the communion trays filled with juice

(Welch's not the real stuff) passed by the old fellow he mistakenly thought it was the offering plate and he tossed a handful of coins into the tray.

I was sitting right behind him and I saw and heard the whole thing. The coins clanged loudly and the juice spilled. You know how it is when something funny happens in church. One's composure is challenged and what little I had at the age of 10 was quickly gone. My buddies and I lost it! Right there in the holy and sacred moment of observing the Lord's Supper I started laughing. So did Rick and Bill. We just could not contain ourselves. Money in the communion tray!

But it got worse—at least for me. The tray weaved its way to the end of the pew in front of me and then made its turn back toward me. We all immediately bowed our heads so as not to look at one another and we slowly composed ourselves. It was hard but we managed. . . until the tray came to me. I slowly gripped the small communion cup, holding it between my fingers. I was back under control and all was well until I bowed my head and casually peered into the cup. To my surprise and utter amusement there was ole Abe Lincoln staring back at me. My cup was the recipient of one of the misplaced pennies! That did it. I snorted, cried, laughed and generally made a fool of myself right then and there. One glimpse of Abe Lincoln in my cup had the rest of the pew laughing and rocking as well.

I was in real trouble but that day but I just couldn't help it. Thankfully my parents understood as I produced a shiny penny and the cup from my pocket that confirmed my dilemma entirely.

And the old man? He later professed faith in Christ and was baptized. It, too, was a rather loud, slushy affair but that is for another time. Every once and a while it is good to remember that laughter does indeed have a place in our world and in God's church.

The Church and the Culture

A RECURRING DEFENSE OF THE EPIC changes that are transpiring in congregational life these days is the cliché "The methods change but the message does not." It is a catchy phrase and one that on the surface provides a plausible defense. For many, that is indeed the case; the message of God has retained credibility and integrity. There is authentic connection with the biblical text and the surrounding culture. The two are held in rightful tension but when "push comes to shove" the text always trumps the culture. That has been the case for orthodox Christianity from the earliest of times. For others, I fear, consumerism, not Christ, is the driving motif for what constitutes a growing congregational life. For them the culture trumps the text. They would never come out and say so, but it is evident in the manner in which they live life and serve. When the text and the culture compete, it is the culture that ultimately rules the day. And what is the ultimate proof for this weak-headed thinking? It, too, is wrapped up in a popular saying, "If it works, do it." That little phrase is what keeps lots of churches in business these days but to what end? Just because it works doesn't necessarily mean it is right! Satan is the best flim-flam pitchman ever, and he knows a thing or two about making things appear to be what they are not.

Several years ago one could legitimately get by with the "methods" versus "message" argument but those days are gone. With the church under full assault from culture, the church must be very wise and sensitive to the power that the culture wields. I see this phenomenon at every turn. Gimmicks and slogans now dominate the pulpits of our land. By "dumbing down" the gospel to make it fit a catchy outline or a slick power-point presentation, we allow cultural impulses to drive what once the gospel did.

Frankly, this whole issue not only fascinates me, it also concerns me. I am no mere observer to the life of the church; I have given my life to it and I continue to serve it in a variety of ways. The gospel cannot be reduced to talking points and snappy sermon starters. The gospel by virtue of its identity will inevitably smack up against the culture that so easily surrounds it. I find very few churches that are authentically wrestling with these implications. Oh, there are those out there that hold fort on the street corners and shout religious slogans at the passersby. These folks are so far removed from culture they have lost the credibility to speak to it. On the other extreme are the voices that can no longer be heard because they have allowed cultural choirs to drown them out. Somewhere in the middle lies a vast host of good people, ministers, and churches that struggle week after week to be true to the God words of scripture while at the same time remaining appropriately connected to a culture that has lost its way and desperately needs to hear from God.

So what do we do? Where do we turn? That is ultimately the foundational question of life. To whom and to what do we call upon to answer our ultimate questions? The Christian community is held together by our core beliefs about the person of Jesus Christ as revealed in Holy Scripture. While there are countless varieties of this expression, at the core is a holy text. That text has stood the test of the ages not by being cutesy and contemporary; rather, it is holy because it speaks different words, challenging words, convicting words, and even haunting words. The text continues to remind us that our Christian journey is to be distinct and different. We are not to fall prey to every gospel gimmick or religious shenanigan. Culture is not Christian. It is as simple as that. And when the culture drives the Christian agenda, something is woefully lacking in our approach and our convictions. A careful reading of Luke's gospel reminds us all that to follow Christ is not cute or fun—it is about faithfulness and loyalty to Christ, even to the cross and even to death. To follow Christ means we are swimming upstream in the culture wars. It is not easy or convenient—it is just the right thing to do.

Debbie

I NEVER CEASE TO BE AMAZED at the people whom God uses. Throughout biblical and human history, God has chosen those who often fit outside of the circle of the elite and the qualified to accomplish His holy work. A quick glance at the roster of biblical of characters will validate this point: Moses, Abraham, Sarah, Peter, John, Mary, and Andrew. Many of these biblical giants did not and would not fit the profile of leader that a "head-hunter" firm might seek.

One of the things that we often miss is that God frequently uses people that the world dismisses. The world's values and priorities are so shallow and empty. The sad but true reality of the situation is that the very things that the world shuns or disavows in persons are the very things that God celebrates in a life.

Debbie was a quite unremarkable young lady by the world's standards. She was born with Down's syndrome, had a serious heart defect, and just did not fit very neatly into society's structure. Nevertheless, She was quite social and was the light of every room she entered.

By the standards of her culture, however, she was never allowed to truly "fit in." Debbie was physically and mentally not capable of holding down a job. Thus many in the schools and most in her town did not truly understand the great potential she possessed.

Her value, however small by society's standard, was immense and great within her church family and the larger Kingdom of God. Her home church did not discard or ignore this precious and gifted young lady. She frequently sang solos, participated in the choir, and worked with mission groups. While Debbie may not have been the most talented person in our church she was certainly the most dedicated.

She worked so hard at everything she did. None of the aforementioned tasks came easily to Debbie. While many of our singers and teachers could sing or teach at the drop of a hat and give a flawless performance, Debbie worked harder and longer than any of them. And when it was her turn to sing a solo, while the tune was often lacking and the words normally muddled, something mystical/magical happened when that precious young lady stepped up to the microphone.

As I look back, I think it was Debbie who first taught me that whether it is singing or teaching or preaching, the very act itself is a sacrifice one makes unto God. When Debbie sang it was clear that she wasn't an entertainer or polished Christian singer. Unlike many of the Broadway wanna-be's that I listen to in church today, Debbie sang her simple song knowing and believing that the tune ascended to the very ears of God.

The difference was simple: Debbie wasn't just singing a song, she was offering a sacrifice. One is for our ears while the other is for God's ears. And every time this precious young lady sang, you just knew that God leaned over the balcony of heaven to hear the sweet sacrifice of song.

Debbie is gone now. She died a young woman. When she died very few people noticed and even fewer truly cared. The world turned its head and said, "She really had nothing to offer us anyway. She was slow. Sick. Incomplete." But the One who matters most knew. He cared. And I have no doubt that when the angels carried this precious soul home, God the Father welcomed her with open arms and a beaming smile. And I bet you he whispered to her, "well done, Debbie, well done. I am so proud of what you accomplished in the short time you lived."

Yes, it is amazing, indeed, the people whom God chooses.

It Is Never Too Late

IN MY TWENTY FIVE YEARS OF MINISTRY what happened two Sunday's ago still has me dumbstruck. It started with an innocent phone call from an eighty-year-old gentleman in the church I serve. He asked if I would be willing to meet with him. I assured him that I could do so and we arranged the time and date.

John (not his real name) and his wife have both been quite ill in recent months and at one time were hospitalized together. As the church does not have a pastor at the time, my guess was that John and his wife were asking if I would be available to conduct their funerals should they die before the church calls a pastor. That was my guess but I could have not been more wrong.

The following Sunday morning John and his wife met with me in the pastor's study of the church. He thanked me for meeting with him and then he began to recount for me the many physical ailments that he and his wife suffer. As they are both so sick John began to develop a picture of the planning he had made with his affairs. He had attended to his will and all other legal matters pertaining to his estate. As he shares this with me I am still guessing that one of the matters he wants to settle is his funeral.

Then it happened. John looked at me and said, "Dr. West I have been a member of this church for over fifty years. I have served on committees and I have been a faithful member. But as I have put my estate in order there was a more important matter that I did not have in order and that was my eternal soul. I have been playing for eighty years and this is too important to play with!"

I was absolutely stunned to hear John's very honest confession. He, indeed, was in church virtually every time the doors opened. But in assessing the final matters of his life he recognized that the issue that mattered more than silver and gold was yet to be attended.

My response was instinctive. I probed a bit with John to ask about the alleged decision made for Christ years prior and I then delved into the movement that led to his ultimate decision.

John's testimony is essentially this: While my earthly affairs were in order the affairs of eternity and of the soul were wholly neglected. At eighty years of age this very humble man made a child-like decision to follow Jesus Christ.

Later that morning John made his decision public with the church. The moment was powerful and spirit filled. There was not a dry eye in the building as I shared with the congregation the momentous decision of John and of the utter courage that he demonstrated by addressing this spiritual matter. It took phenomenal courage for John to stand before a church of which he was a lifetime member and say to them, "after eighty years it is time for me to be honest with you."

I am so grateful that I could be a part of John's story. What a wonderful reminder that our God is never, ever finished with us. Even when we run for eighty years our God still pursues. I am grateful that God finally caught up to John and that John had the guts to let God grab him. For in so doing his affairs are finally in order—those on earth and those in heaven and for that we all give thanks.

It Doesn't Get Any Better Than This
A Tribute to Eve Carson

SEVERAL WEEKS AGO THE STATE of North Carolina, indeed the whole country, was rocked by the senseless and violent murder of University of North Carolina student body president, Eve Carson. It was the lead news story for days as the authorities sought to identify and apprehend the perpetrators of the crime.

Finally, a break came in the case and two suspects were arrested and charged with her murder. Sadly, the rap sheet on the two killers was a mile long. There was gang involvement, repeated arrests and incarcerations, and mishandled probationary supervision. Frankly, the whole scenario is a far too familiar one in the American culture. This tragedy is not unlike other tragedies that cover the headlines of newspapers all across the country every day. It is the same old story. Different town; different victim; same story!

But that is where this story turns from the main path for Eve Carson was no ordinary young lady and her life story is unlike many. She was remarkable, in fact. I did not know her at all but sharing her passion for all things related to the University of North Carolina, I have read tribute after tribute of this sparkling young soul that is no longer among us. In a strange way, I now feel like I knew this young lady very well.

Many of her stories of passion, kindness, and unbridled enthusiasm have captured our imagination but there is one that especially moved me. Eve was a young lady of great pride and tradition. She loved the athletic events at Chapel Hill and regularly attended basketball games. There she sat in the student section of the Dean Dome and cheered her team on to victory. After the games Eve was notorious for quickly making her way down to the arena floor where she would surround herself with her classmates. They would put their arms upon each others shoulders and together they would sing the Alma Mater of North Carolina together. Then Eve would insist that they remain in close ranks for a group photo (which often included some UNC basketball players). After the singing and the photos, Eve did one more thing: she would pull her friends into a huddle, look them in the eye and say: "Guys, look around. Enjoy this. Soak it in. These are the best days of our lives." They were for her; and sadly, her best days among us are no more.

I've been haunted by those words. Though I did not know Eve, the infectious living of her life has been a blessing to me. She was a young lady but she understood the value of time and the brevity of life. Who knows: perhaps she sensed this mystery in life in ways one cannot fully comprehend. She knew something that many of us do not. She knew that life is a gift that God gives us and we are to fully enjoy every minute and every second of our existence.

Her words have been good for me. They have caused me to reconsider some things in my life—how I manage my time, where I invest my energies, in short, what I do with the time God gives me.

Eve's young life and tragic death serve as powerful reminders that we dare not miss the moments of life that truly compose our life. Stop. Look around. These are truly the best moments of our life. They really and truly are. We dare not miss them.

Flea Market Theology

A CAREFUL READING OF THE NEW TESTAMENT can be a daunting thing. Try reading it sometime and you might be surprised what you find there and perhaps even more curiously, what you do not find there. There is a good bit of folklore gospel these days that on occasion directs our churches. Some folks quote "scripture" that are just not there. Others promote not a folklore gospel but a cultural gospel. Reading the Bible through a cultural lens can be very dangerous. Americans are particularly vulnerable to this practice. We wrap our patriotic views around Scripture and force feed conclusions upon a text that is just not there. At last check I am hard pressed to find any evidence indicating that God is registered as an American citizen.

So be warned; reading the New Testament can be a daunting thing. Take the composition of the church, for example. When you read the stories of the followers of Jesus you get a clear picture that the kind of people who follow Jesus today are not at all like those who embarked on the initial Kingdom journey.

Throughout the New Testament Jesus collects the oddest sorts of people to join in the cause. There are the sick and lame ones, the broken and blind ones. It was as if Jesus were walking the countryside looking for the mismatched souls of society.

I guess there is an element of flea-market theology here. Flea markets were born out of our need to get rid of things we no longer want. We might say it is a place to swap junk. In so many ways that is the way Jesus went about his work. He was collecting people that no one else wanted. They were the cast offs and the cast out of this world and it was as if Jesus said, "The more dents and dings you have, the more valuable you are to me."

You cannot read the New Testament without encountering this flea market theology. Which raises, for me at least, a very troubling question for the church today: what happened? What happened?

Why have shifted we from flea market theology to trendy boutique theology. Look around at most of our churches today and the very kind of people that Jesus called and collected along the way are rarely seen and welcomed in the church anymore.

We have so sanitized the gospel it is no Gospel at all. Jesus came to claim and call sinners. Look again at his work. He assembled sick ones, blind ones, broken ones—the kind of people we run from Jesus ran toward.

I have this sick, sinking feeling sometime in the pit of my stomach. Maybe we have missed God's message altogether. Maybe what we call "church" is nothing close to what God expects. Maybe God doesn't even recognize his own church.

Sometimes I wonder about this. I really do. Especially when I read the scary and haunting words of the New Testament and especially when I see how the very ones Jesus embraced are kept at arms length from God's church today.

Our God Has a Thing For Trees

Our God must have a thing for trees. At two decisive and creation shaping moments in history, God positioned a tree in the center of the story. The first tree stood tall and central in the Garden of Eden. In the fresh dew of creation God formed a lovely, appealing tree. The tree was something of a covenant tree. It defined the nature of God's relationship to creation. And while our God offered the bounty of the entire garden to Adam and Eve, he strictly warned that the one tree was "off limits" and was to be avoided at all costs.

God chose a tree, that which grows deep into the soil—the same soil, I might add, from which humans were created—and whose branches reach towards the heaven as if to touch the face of God. This wonderful tree represented God's order in the world. But with childish rebellion we violated the boundaries of the tree and sin fell from it like rain. The eruption of sin into the world occurred in the shadow of this tree.

Centuries passed and the stain of what happened in the garden was etched into every crevice of creation. As the created ones we made a royal mess of everything decent and good that our God had given us.

The cycle continued until one day God introduced his solution to our mess. His solution was Jesus Christ. Born in a barn, a carpenter by trade—a real hammer and nails guy—and one who knew a great deal about trees and wood. Jesus came to reverse the deadly momentum of what had happened under the tree in the Garden.

Ultimately the world seized him, condemned him, and sentenced him to die. His crime? He was guilty of nothing more than extravagant love. But that kind of love will doom you in any era.

And wouldn't you know it? The despairing cycle that started in the shadow of a tree would ultimately end in the shadow of another tree. But it is there that the similarity ends. For this tree was in no garden. This tree was placed on a stony hill that looked like a skull—Golgotha. The hands of God did not create this tree; this tree was stained with the fingerprints of humanity. And while the original tree was a thing of beauty, this tree was ghastly and cold.

Sin erupted from one tree; grace dripped down from another.

Yes, our God has a thing for trees! He chose this wondrous element of creation to demonstrate the depth of his love and mercy.

As we walk toward the week of Passion and remembrance, I pray that each of us will diligently seek to honor the sacrifice and the suffering of the Savior. He spilled his blood. This innocent one gave all so the guilty might live, He offered his blood—his life—for ours. As we walk and as we remember, may it not be said of us that his blood was spilled in vain.

Gimmicks and God

SOMEONE FORGOT TO TELL ME that God is now in the gimmick business. I know that I am busy and miss a lot of things but I did not know that God was now an entrepreneur. It was only recently that I saw his products on the shelf of a local Christian store. Shows how out of touch I am. I didn't even know that God had a marketing director!

Here is the catch: apparently God is now into packing and distributing grace in a kit. For a modest sum you can now purchase all of the spiritual help you need. It must be so for as I walked the aisle of that bookstore I was absolutely astonished at God's merchandise.

Need to lose weight? No, problem—God has a low-fat, low-cal kit just for you! Struggling with guilt? In just twelve weeks you can live a life free from all anxiety and care. Don't believe me? I saw it with my own eyes. Need help with your children? For $49.95 you will be guaranteed to raise children who never raise their voice, make the wrong decisions, or ever cause you to lose a minute of sleep. At the end of the course there is no certificate of completion but the children are awarded personal halos. And if this isn't enough, you can also purchase a kit and a video that will make you more like Jesus. Of course Jesus would want you to buy the three workbooks, video, and special study Bible in order to be successful.

What under God's heaven has happened to us? Have we lost our common sense abilities? The last time I checked the church has relied upon the Holy Scripture to be our sole guide and authority. But from what I am now hearing unless you enroll in the latest study course or read the hottest Christian novel, you are just not getting enough inspiration in your life.

Though my comments are to be received tongue-in-cheek, I pray that you hear the urgency of my words. In less than 30 years we have thumbed our noses at the biblical and theological traditions of the church and said: "we need more than the Bible to satisfy us. Give us god in a kit! Put it on video and it is even better."

When I see the peddlers of grace I often think back to Martin Luther, the great reformer of the church. In his conflict with the papacy one of the precipitating factors in his break from the church was over the matter of the selling of indulgences—the practice of selling forgiveness. Herr Luther would wince at the for-profit (not prophet) madness that has besieged the Christian community.

For 20 centuries the church has survived—indeed thrived—without benefit of gimmick and packaged grace. The reformation of truth of *sola scriptura* (scripture alone) is as applicable today as it was centuries ago.

May God deliver us from consumer grace and restore us to the singular and satisfactory answers contained in his holy Word. And while outside helps are just that, "helps," they should never be considered the primary authority and voice in our lives.

Dead at Forty:
In Memoriam of Daniel E. Goodman

FOUR WEEKS AGO YESTERDAY DEATH came sneaking into our school and robbed us blind. It was an ordinary, uneventful morning. I was in my office early preparing for an eight o'clock class when my cell phone rang. The caller on the other end was our University Minister. His words kicked me in the gut. A treasured friend and office suite mate of mine was being rushed to the hospital and it appeared to be catastrophic. The news knocked my life off balance for a bit. I literally left my office and walked outside for a moment to catch my breath and get my wits about me. How could this be? My friend was a youthful and vivacious forty years old. He was a superb athlete and was remarkably disciplined in his diet and life habits.

Within the hour our worst fears were confirmed; my friend and colleague, Dr. Daniel Goodman, was dead—dead at forty. I, along with another School of Divinity colleague, bore the unenviable task of breaking the horrific, unspeakable news to the remainder of our faculty and students—dead at forty.

The rest of the day was a blur and a whirlwind as we hung on by a thread of faith and hope. We cried together, laughed together, grieved together, prayed together and worshipped together. It was an extraordinary day.

Dan was a "Haley's Comet" type of personality; he was so vivacious and alive. Frankly, I don't know that I have ever met a person with so much spunk and enthusiasm for life. He was part Dennis the Menace and part Jerry Seinfeld. He was mischievous and quirky. And he was brilliant. He was hands down the budding star on our faculty. He was a New Testament scholar and a remarkable participant in Jewish-Christian dialogue efforts. He believed that the Christian community ought to and should learn from our "mother" faith, the heritage of Jesus Christ himself.

One of students likened him to a space shuttle returning to earth. There was always sparks and fire when Goodman took the stage. He had a wicked sense of humor and he was prone to sarcasm when someone offered up foolishness in his class. Dan was not one to tolerate fools. He pushed his students hard to be achievers but more importantly to be thinkers. He had little patience with soft-headed Christianity. He believed that our faith could face up to the hard questions among us and he proved that every day.

The saddest irony of all in this story is Dan's own childhood. He lost his father in a tragic accident when he was a boy. Dan's greatest passion in life was caring for and spoiling his family. In part that passion was fueled by the pain of his own childhood in growing up without a father. That is why he was so compulsive in caring for himself. He verbalized on more than one occasion that he wanted to be there for his two boys and that they would not hurt as he had.

Regrettably and ironically, Dan, like his own father, did not live to be there for his boys either—dead at forty. Yet there is a remarkable hint of grace that we have all witnessed in the days following his death. It is clear that Dan established the proper foundations in the life of his wife and children. In the midst of their deepest sorrow, they have evidenced extraordinary grace and courage. They are holding up just as their beloved husband and father would have desired.

Death is sneaky and cruel. It does not always take those who live long and accomplished lives. Sometimes death sneaks into the most unusual of places. Accordingly, it serves to remind us all to cherish our days, love those among us, enjoy both the rain and sunshine, and cling ferociously to the hand of God. It is a lesson many of us have learned in the wake of one who is dead at forty.

Brother I. M. Right

BROTHER I. M. RIGHT IS AT IT AGAIN. He recently felt led to actively pursue a clandestine campaign to oust his pastor. With the tact the diplomacy of a bulldozer, he secretly called members of his church trying to stir up emotions (and potential votes) against his minister. Brother I.M. is good at this sort of thing. He has personally been in the forefront of the removal of the last four pastors in his church. He is the Baptist equivalent of an assassin and he is quite good at his craft.

Once again Brother Right has pulled out his notoriously big spoon and is stirring things up. He is tired of the pastor and he truly believes it is his God ordained duty to make life so miserable for the pastor and his family that they will finally leave. It has worked for him many times in the past and he believes it will work again.

This time the dispute is not about theology or morality, it is plain and simply about his distain for his pastor. There is no feigned "loving your neighbor as yourself" with I.M.; no, that would be too simple. He hates the man—in the name of God.

What is left unsaid with Brother I.M. is that this behavior is pathological. He is **always** at the center of the congregational storm. Here is how it unfolds: in the first year of a new pastor's tenure, I.M. is the most supportive and helpful person in the congregation. He is friendly and encouraging and he thinks the new pastor can do no wrong. In the second year, the newness of the pastor's tenure begins to wear off and he is seen for what he truly is, just a man—nothing more and nothing less. The humanity of the pastor threatens I.M. and he slowly begins to attack the pastor's weakness with any and all who will listen to him. By the third year, the cycle is reaching epidemic proportions. Brother I.M. Right is "quietly" making phone calls, holding secret meetings, and is plotting the downfall of yet another servant of God.

I have know Brother I.M. all of my life. Strangely, while his name has changed from church to church, I have bumped into either him or his likes everywhere I've been. It was because of the deplorable behavior of his kin in reference to the beloved pastor of my youth that I found it very difficult to respond to God's call to ministry. I had seen first-hand how the "Right Family" treated ministers and I wanted no part of that.

I am embarrassed for the behavior of such people and I am weary of the perpetual conflict that they cause. Moreover, I am weary of the churches that allow this type of abusive behavior to continue. Does no one have the courage or the gumption to stand up to congregational bullies like Brother I.M. and say, "enough is enough!" In all of my years of service to the church I have yet to see anyone stand up to the ecclesial blowhards.

In the meantime I pray for the poor pastor who will serve in I.M.'s church. I know what the poor sucker is in for. And, I pray for Brother I.M. Right. I pray that God will touch his heart, his head, and his attitude before he finally has to answer for his actions.

We Got it Wrong

IN AMERICA OUR MEASURING RODS are all wrong. We measure life, for example, by its length not by its depth or height and that is wrong. We measure wealth by money not treasures and that too is wrong. We mark beauty as that which we see on the outside never once considering the inner quality of the soul. And as a nation we tend to measure our strength by the number of weapons in our arsenal not the character of our people.

The reason our nation has historically been so strong is the depth of the character of its people. I participated in a patriotic service last weekend. It was a moving and humbling experience to share in tribute to a generation of citizens who gave so freely and so sacrificially to our nation.

As I watched these aging men and women slowly make their way to the front of the auditorium, I couldn't help but measure their character and courage. Many of these souls fought during World War II, the Korean conflict, and Vietnam. I saw a depth of spirit that I rarely see anymore. And though I am not a natural weeper, I must confess that the sight of these old patriots brought a lump to throat and a tear to my eye. They are from a different generation with a deeper sense of value and loyalty than we currently find in the post-modern world.

Many of these souls are the same age of my father. I know of his patriotism but I also know of his character. And I know, that though my father is not educated, he does not allow his love for his country to cloud the judgment of his country. He asks questions, on occasion, that make me proud. He knows that America is often not guided by principles of justice and righteousness but by greed and self-interest. He sometimes sees the larger picture that is at stake in our nation. And while he agrees with Tom Brokaw in naming his era as the Greatest Generation, he also knows that his generation dropped the ball on the issue of racial justice and equality. He knows that, accepts that, and is not proud of that.

The true character of a nation is found in the trenches of ordinary lives that believe in justice for all—not just those with whom they agree. That kind of justice truly rests in the hearts of the godly. Justice for many in our culture is simply defined as retaliation against an aggressor. "We will bring them to justice," we say, and rightly so.

But what about justice not simply for the aggressor but justice on behalf of the oppressed and the downtrodden? What about justice for the child that is lost in a heavily bureaucratic foster care system? Do we pursue justice for her? What about justice for those who are racially and economically oppressed? Do we ring the bell of justice on their behalf?

On this significant national holiday let us not forget those who fought and died for our country. Their sacrifice so great dare not be in vain. We owe it to their memory to fight hard for all people in all places so that "justice will flow down like a river." May it flow this holiday and every day. Amen

Kingdom Eyes

HAVE YOU EVER WORN 3-D glasses? The first time I used them I was at Disneyworld with my family. We went to a 3-D movie. The movie started and at that moment I was not wearing my glasses. When I slipped them on, however, the most amazing things happened. The otherwise drab images on the screen suddenly exploded to life. And there were things happening on the screen that only the glasses revealed. Butterflies flew into my face. A little bird chirped at the end of my nose. I even ducked when an eagle soared right toward me. I had so much fun that day taking my glasses on and off to see the difference they made.

As a Christian I am still taking the glasses on and off. Sometimes I look around at the world and think, "What a wonderful place this is. But then I slip my Kingdom glasses on and I am reminded that what I see in this world is not nearly as important as what I see there."

In Luke's gospel (10: 17-24) there is a wonderful account of the return of the 70 from their first mission. They were so excited to return and report their experiences to Jesus. They were like children at an Easter egg hunt! With breathless joy they reported that they had never experienced or seen anything like this before. "Lord," they said, "even the demons are subject to us in your name." Until this time they had only seen the "stuff" of this world; but in the power of Christ they saw the other world. It was as if they had 3-D glasses.

If you have not seen *The Chronicles of Narnia* you have missed a treat and a blessing. The movie is based upon the writings of C.S. Lewis. The story is about four children who are forced to leave their London home in World War II.. The children live in a country estate and while living there they engage in the childhood game of hide 'n seek. Lucy, the youngest, tries to find a suitable hiding place and she stumbles upon an abandoned wardrobe. She opens the door to hide from her brother and while in the wardrobe she stumbles into another world called Narnia.

I think that is what happened to the disciples. When they returned from their mission it was as if they had stumbled into an altogether different world. They saw things differently. They heard things differently. Everything was different. It is what Jesus said, to his followers. He said, "You have been blessed to see what others cannot see." Things were different because they were now seeing through Kingdom eyes.

And what is that difference? It is really quite simple. Earthly eyes can only see things as they are. Kingdom eyes see things as they can become. It is what Jesus specialized in. Jesus did not see fishermen, tax collectors, prostitutes; Jesus saw people. He saw people through Kingdom eyes and it made all the difference in the world. . . and for those among us with the eyes to see, it still does.

Bigger Ain't Always Better

SOMEWHERE ALONG THE LINE WE HAVE missed something in the American Christian culture. This point was driven home to me in a recent dialogue in which the changes inherent to many churches were the point of discussion. It does not take a rocket scientist to recognize that changes of seismic proportion are underway in our culture and in our churches. That emphasis did not catch me off guard at all but what did surprise and offend me was the focus on what constitutes authentic church and where the notion of size fits into that conversation.

One minister in particular got under my skin with his idea that "authentic" church is predicated on the notion that "bigger is always better." He hammered this point across wherein he all but said, "Small churches no longer have a role and an appropriate place in the changing religious landscape." For him, at least, "real" churches have adopted the philosophy of municipal government—the church is to provide all of the services to its community so that it becomes an entity all unto itself. It is the theological equivalent of a Wal-Mart supercenter! Everything one needs is housed under the same roof. To believe that churches are like that is the height of arrogance and self-righteousness for what follows is a natural conclusion: our church has all of the answers and all of the necessary services; if your church does not, then you are not authentic. I would want to be careful to not misrepresent the dialogue but that it is the essence of what was said.

Frankly, that kind of philosophy smacks at the heart of what is wrong in most religious circles. In almost thirty years of ministry to the church, and as one who works closely with multiple religious contexts now, I am increasingly convinced that our standards for Kingdom measurements are all wrong. In the vast majority of congregational settings, what constitutes success is based solely upon secular/corporate standards. In laymen's terms it is **only** about "nickels and noses"—how many people were there and how much money came in? Think about that philosophy. That sounds more like Wall Street than the Kingdom of Heaven and yet those are the precise terms used in most churches I know.

That is why I propose a radical reversal for gauging congregational success. Rather than measuring the height of the steeple, why not measure the depth of the people? It the very thing that the Willow Creek mega church in Chicago did several years ago. In many ways they are the prototype for mega churches and were doing it so long before others caught on. The Willow Creek community has generated countless thousands of participants and has hauled in millions and millions of dollars. But to what end? Their own recent studies reveal that while their secular measure of success was stellar—lots of nickels and noses—they were doing a lousy job of developing disciples. I applaud their honesty. I wish others would follow.

It is time for churches to go back to the basics: ministering to the least of these, loving their neighbor, developing genuine disciples for Christ, and making a real difference in the community, one person at a time. Any church can do this and every church should do this. Assembly line ministry is not going to cut it much longer.

Smoke and mirrors will continue to attract the crowds, but crowds do not equate to disciples. Just because people and money are there in no way means that

God is! That is something for all of us—especially in the church to think about.

The Messy Notion of 'Mission' Trips

Finally I have found a church that just might understand its mission. In my current interim one of the things that the little church does on an annual basis is mission's week. In most churches "mission week" means that the members of the church go to another community, state, or country on a "mission trip." Mission trips have become very popular in the modern church. They provide valuable experiences for both those who serve and those who are served. But in virtually every situation that I know, the theology behind the mission is a faulty one.

Faulty, you ask? In what way? Typically the mission trip experience is conducted away from home. Even more typical is the lack of "at home" mission experience or exposure that most participants have prior to the event. Something is biblically wrong when persons step over local needs in order to travel to other communities to minister. There is nothing wrong with mission moments; they are indeed what the Kingdom is about. But the way most of us conduct mission trips is horribly wrong.

One of the saddest things I ever heard in ministry involved a minister that once called me about a mission opportunity and the primary criteria for the trip was that it needed to be a place where the youth could "pack their bathing suits." His mission objective was abundantly clear; the mission was to have fun and squeeze a little God into the experience.

All of this is to share the vision and mission of this little church in North Carolina. They have strategically (and biblically) decided that before they ever take their church on a "mission trip" they will invest several years in a "home" mission trip. What a refreshing and biblically solid approach. After all when the church was launched the mission was to move from Jerusalem (home) to Samaria (beyond home) to the ends of the earth.

So this church has followed the biblical template. They are honing their mission and ministry skills at home. They treat the entire week like a mission experience. They work from sunup to sundown and then they go home. But their mission is done in the community around them.

I was so impressed with what I saw. Over sixty people committed to this mission. And at the end of the week the results were staggering. They had visited countless persons in the community, assisted in valuable ways, and most important, they bore witness to Christ in the efforts.

I am convinced that what they are doing is correct. One of these years in the very near future they have plans to "go to the ends of the earth." But they won't dare do that until they have ministered in their Jerusalem.

Wouldn't you hate to stand before God one day and be asked, "Why were you so busy in "the ends of the earth" when you did not take your responsibility to family and neighbor seriously?

I'm glad to see that after many years of ministry service, I have finally met a church that has it right. I pray there will be others that quickly follow.

My Daddy

MY LIFE AND MINISTRY ARE about words. I use them in my teaching and in my preaching. Sometimes, however, there are no words. Sometimes the silence speaks more powerfully and more compellingly than our puny attempts to break the silence with ill-placed words. Such has been my observation over the course of the last three months.

In mid August my father became seriously ill. Since that time my life has been on hold and I attempted to close the distance between North Carolina and Virginia with regular trips to assist in my father's care. In that context it was with great sorrow and profound gratitude that I stood with my daddy as he drew his last breath on October 19th. His death was not unexpected. We knew it was imminent. Even more amazingly, he knew it too. The day prior to his death my father perceptively noted for us that some things were changing in his condition. I don't know how he knew but he knew. It was typical of my dad, really; he was trying to prepare us in advance of what he knew was coming. It was his way, even in death, to try to help us and to comfort us.

As a minister I am typically on the giving end of ministry to the grief stricken. I know how to visit the dying and how to offer hope to the bereaved. I am comfortable in that role; I was far less comfortable to be on the receiving end. I wanted to do something but there was little I could do. I let my family and the family of God minister to me and I can honestly say that while some attempts were technically incorrect, the attempts could not have been more sensitive and loving. I have been overwhelmed and humbled by the response my family and I have received.

I presided over my father's funeral. Many have commented on the courage it took to do such a thing. To the contrary, it was not courageous at all; it was just the right thing to do. I was really the only one who could appropriately sum up the legacy of my dear father. I could not allow someone else to preach a "fill in the blank" funeral message for my father. I have endured too many of those horrific approaches to ministry and I was not about to allow my dad's life to be reduced to a few generic words, a poem and a prayer. So tough or not to do my father's service was, for me, the right thing.

My father was not an educated man. Regrettably, my father had to quit school in the seventh grade to go to work and help support the remainder of his brothers and sister. He was never able to return. I hate that for him because he was a very bright and intelligent soul. What he lacked in formal education he more than made up for in common sense and good old fashioned ingenuity.

I am a teacher and preacher by trade but in my father's last moments he taught me lessons that I pray I will never forget. With my father's condition he was heavily oxygenated requiring two masks to live. He was so short of breath that he could not breathe properly and he certainly could not speak. You could tell when daddy was about to speak. He would take several deep breaths, lift the mask, and then attempt to talk. One thing remained constant, though; my dad insisted on offering the blessing for his food. Even with no breath he offered a prayer of thanks for his food—food incidentally, that he would not be able to eat.

I learned a lesson I will never forget. Never take another breath of life for granted and always remember to thank God. My dad taught me that lesson and even in his dying that lesson is a part of my being. Life is a gift from God. It is never to be taken for granted. As I. . .we go forward. . . the experiences of life and death are all around us. What we learn from them and how we incorporate them into our living is utterly our decision. As for me I have chosen anew to learn something. Thank you, daddy, for all that you taught me. There is a hole in my heart that will be there forever. But I plan to plug that hole with the good memories of your life and with the lessons you taught me both in life and in death. I pray that will hold me over until I see you again someday.

Counting the Pocket Change

I HAVE RECENTLY BEEN TRYING TO SPEND time with a dear friend and colleague whose wife is dying of cancer. Just months ago this very vibrant and active person (and former world class athlete) showed no signs of illness. Then one day "out of the blue" she came down with a fever and has been in a life and death battle with cancer ever since.

Following multiple surgeries and a brutal course of chemotherapy, her physical condition is still quite unstable and her prognosis not good. To her credit she has not given in at all. In fact 10 days following her surgery, she was back in the classroom trying to conduct her classes. On the days between her chemotherapy treatments she can be found in her office and teaching her class. But her condition continues to deteriorate and if God does not intervene, her death will come soon.

Her husband is close friend of mine. He, too, is a minister and I have found that those of us in the ministry are often very hard to minister to. We know the ropes too well and the defense mechanisms that we are forced to develop to survive in ministry quickly rise to the surface. Nevertheless, I have attempted to provide prayerful and pastoral presence. Last week in a very brief conversation with him, he said something that accurately describes, for him, the life stage he finds himself in. He said to me, "Danny, with all that my family is facing right now, I don't have time to worry about 'pocket change.'"

His meaning could not have been clearer. His wife is dying. His children are losing a mother and their grandchild will grow up without the love a grandmother. In that crisis state of anticipatory grief and sorrow, my friend is not worried about rising gasoline costs and whether his favorite football team wins or loses. Those things, for him, are but "pocket change" and he is focused on the primary concerns of his life.

I could never speak for another soul but my hunch is that if my friend were to unpack all of his emotions in this difficult hour he would clearly say, "My priorities have finally shifted into high gear for the first time in my life." I have seen that in him. Though he is greatly distracted and walks through life in a fog, there is also an unusual and heightened sense of awareness present in his life.

What I think I am seeing is this. His focus is squarely centered upon the essentials of life. The periphery doesn't matter now. Pocket change is inconsequential. It is now about tending to a dying wife and squeezing every drop of life and love out of this painful moment.

Most of us learn our lessons the hard way, don't we? We wait until crisis hits before we discard the "pocket change" and focus on the primary currency of our life. Perhaps my friend's example can awaken those of who struggle with priority and balance in life to learn the important lessons while we can and when we can. The holy life that God gives to us is too important to squander it on "pocket change."

Prodigal Preaching

IN THE LAST THREE YEARS I HAVE LISTENED to a lot of sermons. One of my responsibilities at Gardner-Webb is to teach preaching. I enjoy the teaching and instruction of young preachers but listening to some of their efforts can be a painful experience.

The most common problem that I see is one that only experience can conquer and that is good old-fashioned stage fright. Lots of folks struggle with a fear of public speaking and preachers are not immune to that. But the problems run deeper than sweaty palms and cotton mouth speakers; many of the problems come from the role models many young preachers emulate.

I listen to a lot of "prodigal preaching." Prodigal preaching is preaching that greedily wanders from the homeland of the biblical text into the far country of excess. There the prodigal preacher "wallows" for a while and in desperation makes a last ditch effort to return home. When I hear prodigal preaching—which I sadly hear all of the time both in class and on television-- I reach for a Goody's headache powder because the suffering is intense and it needs fast action relief.

I know where these students get lost in their preaching; they have listened to misguided practices for years. And what really froths me are those loud mouthed proclaimers who spend twenty minutes telling you that you are about to hear "true biblical preaching" when the "sermon" is nothing more than a tirade against some social ill or is a platform to coax the listener to vote a particular way. The prodigal sermon has nothing to do with the biblical text but rather is a soapbox moment for the preacher to spout his own opinions.

One of the best truths I learned about preaching came from the pen of Tom Long, a preaching professor in Atlanta who said, "The pulpit is above all things a witness stand." It is not a place to air personal opinion and ignorance. It is the place where the preacher declares what the text has to say and nothing else. Tell the truth, the whole truth, and nothing but the biblical truth! But don't "make up" biblical truth in order to fit personal agendas.

One of the most horrific prodigal sermons I heard was from a student who had merely borrowed what he heard a popular "biblical preacher" offer in a minister's conference. The biblical text was from Mark 2 but the biblical text does not "get in the way" in prodigal preaching. The text is parenthetical to the sermon! This particular sermon tells of the paralyzed man who cannot get to Jesus so his innovative friends cut a whole in the roof and lower the man into the house where Jesus was. The prodigal sermon I heard somehow found its way to a prosperity gospel and the healed one arose to great riches and wealth because of his faith. There is not one mention of wealth and success in that passage. Not one! And yet that was the focal point of the prodigal sermon. When I challenged the young preacher he defensively said, "Well that is what brother so and so says." My response was swift and firm—but that is NOT what the biblical text says.

Preaching is a sacred task; too sacred to allow prodigal preachers to preach prodigal sermons. One rule of thumb for gauging solid preaching is not the rhetoric, alliteration, or gimmick that the preacher employs. There is one simple rule: is the sermon a mirror of the biblical text? If not the sermon has strayed into the far country and only grace (and hard work) will allow it to return home.

Learning to Pull Over

LAST WEEKEND WAS AN IMPORTANT ONE for me. I have been "under the gun" since August so I took some important time to get away and relax. There is no better place in the entire world for me than the mountains. As I drove to Asheville for the weekend (I didn't have time to enjoy the REAL mountains of Tennessee), several times I pulled over to enjoy the spectacular scenery that God had created that weekend. God was at his best! The colors from his easel were spectacular. I saw wonderful reds and yellows. The view was breathtaking. It is one thing to enjoy the beauty while driving through; it is an altogether different thing to enjoy the beauty while sitting still.

Those "pullover moments" are for me a metaphor for entering the Thanksgiving season. I need those specially selected moments and places to help me better appreciate the world around me. I suspect that I am not alone in this assessment. My life is too busy and my calendar is too full. If I am not careful, I allow the busyness of my world to become the pattern for my life. Left unchallenged, my life is too complicated to rightly appreciate all that is around me. I need to pull over for a moment. I need to slow down. If I don't slow down I will miss the splendor of the world around me and the richness of the relationships that I enjoy.

The truth is all of us need to do that. Thanksgiving is one of those holy moments on the calendar wherein we are granted permission and even encouraged to slow down to enjoy the world around us. Thanksgiving cannot be processed in the fast lane. It demands that we slow down, pull over, and sit a spell.

It is while "sitting a spell" that we typically do our best work. It is in that mode of reflection that the important matters are attended. I need to "pull over" occasionally and consider my God. God has blessed my life in immeasurable ways. I sometimes stop to consider how fortunate I am and I have to pinch myself. My life is not nor ever has been perfect; I have made more than my fair share of mistakes and I have tasted the bitter tears of pain and death. I do know what it is to hurt. In spite of that, as I look back over the path of my life, I have known far greater joy than sorrow. God has been amazingly gracious and kind to me over the years of my life. In fact everything that really counts for me all goes back to God.

When I "sit a spell" I also find the time to do my best work with my family. Again, it is God that has smiled upon me in the form of family. It started with my wonderful and loving parents. I owe God such a debt of gratitude for placing me in the loving arms of my parents. I could not have had a better home. In addition, I have been blessed with a wonderful wife and three remarkable, almost-perfect, children. They have all enriched my life in ways that I cannot adequately describe. Their presence in my world has only made me a better person. If I am not careful, my frenetic schedule prohibits me from slowing down enough to enjoy them.

I am also grateful for a challenging and nurturing culture in which I now work. I could never have imagined as a young minister that God would actually allow me to teach in a Seminary setting. On occasion several of us on the faculty will look at each other and ask, "How did we land such a wonderful and challenging gig?" I am actually granted the grace to help teach and encourage young ministers. Opportunities like this are truly rare; not many people get to do what I get to do. I don't understand how/why I came to this place but I am profoundly grateful to God for the privilege. Others, I know, are better qualified in some ways but God placed me here. It is a good place to be. It is even better when I "pull over" and consider the honor that I enjoy.

Be careful out there this Thanksgiving season. Don't go so fast that the important stuff of life is overlooked. Slow down. If need be, pull over; don't miss out on all that this holy season has to offer. It is by design, I think, that as we begin to slow down in the season of thanks, we place ourselves in a rightful position to appreciate the most bountiful gift of all—Jesus the Christ. I pray that God's most wonderful grace and bounty will be upon us all this coming season.

Racism and the Church

IN SERVICE TO THE CHURCH ONE ULTIMATELY must develop a thick skin and the ability to let things pass through your spirit or the work will eventually kill you. I must admit that even after many years of ministry I find myself somewhere between the position of not letting criticism bother me at all and allowing it to hurt terribly. Typically, I have learned to handle criticism and most of the time it does not bother me anymore.

I have been blessed in my ministry to not be on the receiving end of harsh and inappropriate criticism on a regular basis. I've had my moments as have all of us. But I thank God that I have not lived as some ministers have under the constant barrage of criticism and harshness.

Like all ministers I have been on the receiving end of tongue lashings, angry outbursts, and inappropriate actions. Sadly, it goes with service to the church. But in all of my years I have never experienced what I encountered at a church in North Carolina several years ago. In my message I quoted from a wonderful film entitled "Glory" that features the all black 54th brigade that fought in the Civil War. There is a wonderful scene in the movie in which the black soldiers gather by a campfire on the eve of a momentous battle and they are preparing their hearts for war and for death. It is a testimony scene and in it the character played by the great Morgan Freeman declares, "Let our children know that if we fall, we fell standing up." It is a powerful claim that can easily apply to the Christian faith and our need to stand for some things. I built my comments from that testimony and reminded the church that in so many areas the church has been sitting, not standing for the right things. Among them is the issue of race relations.

I can truly say it was a memorable service and one in which I had an inordinate number of parishioners in line to speak with me. I guess I was swept up in the moment because "he" caught me off guard. I did not know the very distinguished looking gentleman waiting in line to speak with me. I do now! He looked me in the eye and proceeded to scream at me that he never thought he would hear someone defend and I quote, "The Yankee aggression upon the South and a desecration of the confederate heritage." For a moment I was not only stunned but confused. Who uses that kind of language in the twenty-first century? It is relic language and as I would soon discover, purely racist language. He continued the verbal assault on the steps of the house of God by saying things like, "blacks and their place, and the nobility of the Southern cause."

Finally, I preempted the harangue and said, "I am sorry you are so angry, but you must know that you are angry at the wrong person. This is not about the north or the south; it is not about black and white. This is a matter of the Kingdom of God and I will stand fully behind my beliefs for they are biblical and not cultural. If you have a problem, take it up with God, not me"

In that moment I felt so sorry for the gentleman's family. His wife and children were ashamed of their racist father. They were humiliated by his actions and words and they tried so desperately to get away. He turned red in the face and said, "I guess I should not argue with a preacher at church and walked away."

By that afternoon something happened in this church and in my relationship with them. Though I did nothing radical or revolutionary, in their eyes I became a hero because, as I later discovered, this guy was indeed an avowed racist and he had propagated his racist myths for years unchecked in the church.

I was more sad than angry that day from my encounter. The sadness remains for me in knowing that the church continues to harbor racist thoughts and ideology. God's great Kingdom is not black or white or red or blue. Those definitions are attributable to the human condition and they are not at all of God. God created all persons! God loves all persons! And if we are to be in genuine fellowship with him we must strive to do the same. Perhaps the words of Holy Scripture best sum up my convictions: "He who says he is in the light and hates his brother is in the darkness still. . . he who hates his brother is in the darkness and walks in the darkness. . . because the darkness has blinded his eyes." (I John 1: 9-10)

Raking Leaves:
Ministry as Cleaning Up the Messes of Others

LAST WEEK I PERFORMED MY ANNUAL fall ritual of raking leaves and picking up branches. I don't really mind yard work but this one is hard to keep on top of. As soon as one tree drops it leaves another quickly follows. This year, however, I made a concerted effort to keep on top of the leaves so that they did not get out of hand. I am proud to report I have done so. As soon as one tree emptied I was virtually underneath it catching the leaves as they fell. For the first time in years I am not inundated with leaves that pile up so high I can not manage them.

But there is a problem with the leaves. Actually I need to be more specific; there is a problem with my neighbor's leaves. They keep blowing into my yard. Mind you I've kept up with **my** leaves but now I find myself keeping up with my neighbor's leaves that blow into my yard. The homes on either side of me have trees that are on their property but whose leaves fall on my yard. So after cleaning up all of my leaves, I now enjoy cleaning my neighbor's leaves too!

As I was cleaning up someone else's mess last week, it dawned on me that all of my life is given to raking the leaves of others. In some ways as I raked and blew my neighbor's leaves it became a metaphor moment. It summed up my vocation and my calling. Ministry is about that very thing. Ministry is about helping other people straighten out the mess they make of life. Every day of my life in some manner or the other, I find myself helping other people clean up their messes. They are not my messes, mind you, but the messes of others. Nonetheless, I am frequently called upon to help them straighten things up.

I really don't mind it but sometimes it becomes overwhelming. Sometimes I don't have the energy to keep my own yard clean much less the yard of others. That is the great challenge and burden of ministry. And it is the very reason ministers are bailing out of vocational ministry at a record pace.

Just this morning I was visiting with several young ministers and this very issue of self-care and protection was the topic. One of the great threats to ministry is that too often we care for the "leaves" of others and we have not time left to attend to ourselves. Burnout is an ongoing problem for vocational ministers and it is easy to see why. Studies indicate that the average pastor works 65-70 hours per week and even then many feel they have not done enough.

As a reminder to younger ministers I frequently caution them to read the story of Jesus and his ministry. There were strategic times in his work when he needed to step aside from the burdens and pressure of ministry to simply find quiet time. If it was necessary for Jesus it is certainly needed for the rest of us. Because things have not and they will not changed in ministry.

People will continue to make horrific mistakes and families will constantly face a barrage of assaults. In those moments of crisis they typically bring their "mess" to a counselor or minister. As a minister, it does us little good to be raking the leaves of others, when our yard is full of debris. We must make time for ourselves. It is then and only then that we can best attend to the needs and struggles of others.

Random Thoughts about Kingdom Service

WHILE TRAVELING THIS PAST WEEK ON business, I spent lots of time behind the wheel to ponder things in life. Since my world revolves around the church and the ministry, I could not help but think of things that I observe. Some of these random thoughts are about things that I appreciate; others involve the annoyances that I encounter along the way. As I reflected on these things, I found my list growing longer and longer. In no particular order, and with no particular theme, I share my random thoughts about life in the church.

Random thought number one: I was in a revival several weeks ago and for the first time I can recall in years, we sang the third verse of the hymns. I feel sorry for the third verse. Is it not important, too? If it weren't deemed important by the hymn writer, he or she would not have written it? Where do get off changing the rhythm, message, and structure of perfectly good hymns? Sing all of the words to all of the hymns. I promise it will add only two minutes to the length of the service and it will be worth it.

Random thought number two: How come so many preachers have those "preacher haircuts?" Is there a barber shop etiquette that I don't know about? Is there an unwritten rule on how to fix hair that is being taught and no one told me? I can spot a preacher a mile away not because of a Bible but by the way the hair is combed back or by the application of grease that slicks it down.

Random thought number three: Does no one in the church know how to operate a sound system? I preach in all kinds of settings both large and small and they have one thing in common—the microphones never work properly. They are either too loud, too soft, or they feedback to the extent that the congregation covers their ears. One that especially annoys me is the sound that comes when speaking wherein the speaker sounds like he/she has a bucket over their head. I have come to hate those things! They are distracting to the speaker and the listener and I sure wish someone could figure out how to make them work.

Random thought number four: This one is closely linked to number three. How come Christians cannot spell? Increasingly churches are relying on power point projectors to project choruses, announcements, sermon points, etc. onto a screen. And it would appear that no one in control knows how to spell or proofread. I have seen Christ spelled "Chrisst." I have seen Bible spelled "Bibel." Not long ago I saw the grand old hymn "Blessed Assurance" demoted to " Blessed Issurance." These mistakes are happening inside the church. Church signs are for public display and they can be worse. I actually saw a church sign that read "Are you a Christion?" My inner response was, "No, I can honestly say I am not one of those." I know it takes a little longer to proof read these things, but better to invest in doing it right than investing in cleaning up embarrassments later.

I could go on but I won't. I just have these random thoughts that sometimes make perfect sense to me and to others. Sometimes, however, they only make sense to me. I guess that is why they are mine and they are random.

Restaurant Behavior

A FRIEND RECENTLY SHARED A CONVERSATION he had with a member of his church community. The church member happens to be a waitress in a restaurant in his home town. One day the lady stopped by the church and asked if she could speak with my friend and her pastor. He gladly welcomed her. After exchanging pleasantries, the lady awkwardly broached the reason for her visit.

My friend said it was evident that something was deeply troubling the lady. Finally, she came clean with her burden. Her struggle was with the manner in which her fellow church members and Sunday lunch customers were behaving. One incident in particular stood out. The waitress shared what happened to a colleague of hers that day. At a recent Sunday lunch there was some small error in the delivery of the order. It was very trivial and involved a mix up between green beans and corn. It was the kind of thing that is easily corrected. Instead of gently informing the waitress of the error, a meticulously dressed "gentleman" proceeded to berate her quite loudly in front of the entire restaurant. The poor lady was reduced to tears. As she tearfully went to the back of the restaurant to retrieve his beloved green beans, she painfully wondered aloud, "I wonder what church HE went to today?"

As the waitress recalled this episode with her pastor, he had a sickening feeling that he knew why she was there. She asked him one of the most painful questions he's ever faced in ministry: "Pastor, I was humiliated because I knew what church he attended. I was ashamed to tell my friend that he was a member of my church. Can you please tell me why people who worship God on Sunday morning can be so rude and thoughtless just one hour later? And to make it worse, she said, Sunday tips are the worst we receive all week."

The minister attempted to provide clarity and insight in the situation but there was really nothing he could say or do to defend or vindicate the actions of the church member. He was equally embarrassed and appalled at the actions of one of his own.

One of the recurring threads of critique in the Christian community is that of our sometimes mean and critical spirit. I, too, have witnessed these restaurant and public moments where alleged Christians behave in a rude and offensive manner. What is there about us that causes us to act in such a manner? How can we leave church and the worship of God and in a matter of minutes deteriorate into angry and venomous fools? Frankly, I am weary of that kind of hypocrisy of spirit. I am tired of Christians treating those around them like dirt. I am weary of the anger, the attitude, and the falseness of it all.

When my pastor friend recalled this account the pain in his eyes was visible. He was angry and embarrassed. He was so angry that he tried to have the waitress tell him who the offender was. Rightly (or wrongly) she simply said she would rather not get caught up in that kind of confrontation and refused. My friend said, "What really scares me now is that I cannot think of just one person in my church that would do such a thing, I can think of a countless number of them for I have seen many of them in action."

Think about that. There were so many potential offenders in his congregation he could not figure it out. I wish that my friend's church were the exception but they are not. His church is no worse than most of our churches. There are equal opportunity offenders everywhere I go.

I am saddened and angry that this kind of obnoxious behavior continues. Parenthetically, I am even more outraged when I hear how regularly those of us in ministry treat persons rudely. Ministers can be as rude as anyone else.

I'm not sure why I'm even writing these words today. I guess I've had it with rude, obnoxious, arrogant, boorish "Christians." Maybe in the writing of these words I will become more aware of my own tendencies and imperfections. And, maybe, in the writing I will remind those among us who are prone to abrasive and non-Christian attitudes to seek another path and to start treating those around us in the manner that we desire to be treated. It seems like I recall someone once said "Do unto to others as you would have them do unto you." It was good advice then; it is even better advice today.

The Need to Rest

IT IS MORE THAN A WANT IN MY LIFE these days. It is a need. And the need was met for my family and I last week. We escaped to the beach. With books, lounge chairs and little more crammed into our family van, we made our way to the Outer Banks of North Carolina.

I must say it was a thrill to get away from the telephone, meetings, and the over abundance of commitments that crowd my calendar. As we hit the road driving toward the ocean I could feel my spirit relaxing with each passing mile. Upon my arrival I dropped my bags (and my burdens) and went to stand on the shores of the majestic Atlantic Ocean. Closing my eyes and listening to the incomparable sound of the surf, I knew that I was in the presence of almighty God. I was! It is God's ocean, God's beach, and I am God's child. His presence could not have been more real.

Part of the appeal, for me at least, is that when I am in the presence of the ocean I know that I am confronted with something much larger than myself. So many things in my world are too small to command my attention. And yet it seems that it is the small, petty things that occupy so much of my time. All of us need to occasionally be in the company of that which is beyond ourselves. That is why I enjoy the ocean so. It is big. It is noisy. And no human force can control it. Anne Lamott describes the sound of the ocean as that of a larger than life washing machine. To sit by the water's edge and listen to the thunderous power of God's surf is the kind of therapy and relaxation I need.

Moments of rest are far too few for most American's today. We work long hours and labor under too much stress. It has always been so for the human family but something has shifted in our day that we have lost altogether. Lost in our ambition and drive to be successful or prosperous is the need to find adequate rest and relaxation.

God in his infinite wisdom reminded us of the importance of rest. He named it Sabbath. Sabbath is the time to withdraw from ordinary activity and to allow the breath of God to refresh and mend us. Even the Genesis account of creation reminds us that God took time away from his creative activity to rest.

We have lost the ability to rest. Though our culture is full of recreational centers and our lakes are crowded with pleasure crafts, there is still a gaping hole in many a soul that has lost the ability to inhale the refreshment of Sabbath.

I must admit that I thoroughly enjoyed my time away. I rested. My tattered and frayed spirit was given time to heal. The great Mender of souls took the time to not only wash the mighty waves upon the shores of the beach but he also took the time to wash over my soul with refreshment, encouragement, and rest.

Most of us move too many non-negotiable matters around in our life. I pray that you won't move the matter of rest from your weary life. We all need it. God has always desired it. What a wonderful combination.

Appreciating a Season of Silence

THE WRITER OF ECCLESIASTES OFFERS tremendous wisdom to the modern listener. He reminds us that there is a season for all things in life. One of those things is silence. There is a time to be silent and a time to speak. As a columnist I have been "silent" for a while and it has been good for me. I traveled this summer, I worked this summer, I performed my son's wedding this summer, and while I preached virtually every Sunday, there was a sense in which I was silent in many other ways.

Now, it is time to break the silence again. I remind my students that before any of us dare preach or teach we need to listen long enough to have something to say. I learned that lesson from a powerful (and classic) little book entitled, *A Little Exercise for Young Theologians* by Helmut Thielicke. In this important work, the author reminds young ministers that before they can speak, they must listen. In fact, one of his most famous arguments is that young preachers ought to be discouraged to preach for a season so that they learn something. Many of my students vehemently disagree with that assessment. Having heard many of them preach the silence would have been a blessing to me!

While I have missed writing this summer and remaining connected to the beloved hills of East Tennessee, I must admit that it was good to take some time to listen. Listening is one of the least cultivated gifts in our world. Most of us are adept at speaking. We talk too much. Words surround us to the point we are in verbal overload all the time. What we don't do is listen very well.

I fear that that gift is one that is particularly hard for many Christians. Ours is a verbal faith. We have a story to tell and a witness to bear. But silence is a powerful teacher as well. Frankly, some of my most important life lessons came not from words but in moments of silence. For in the silence I wasn't listening to my verbal outputs or the language of others, I was listening solely to God. Indeed the Bible reminds us that God speaks in a "still small voice." How, in heaven's name, are we to hear that voice when the messy noise of our life drowns out the voice of God?

Several years ago while serving in a church, we tried on a moment of silence as a part of the worship experience.

There was quite an interesting response. The overall response was not favorable. Folks were uncomfortable with the silence. They came to church, they said, to be fed and to worship. They didn't come for silence. What they didn't understand is that silence is a necessary ingredient in worship. We have misled people if they think that singing and preaching are the only components of worship. They are but a part of it. Silence ought to be, too!

As for me, the season of silence is over. I am back at it both in a written and speaking ministry. It is who I am and I enjoy it. But I must confess, I will look forward to next season of silence when it comes my way.

Serendipity

IT IS ONE OF MY FAVORITE WORDS. It is fun to say out loud and it is even more fun to experience. The word? It is serendipity. Serendipity is a wonderful word that refers to those unexpected and unanticipated moments of grace that come to us in life. It speaks to the good surprises in life. Some surprises are not pleasant at all. They announce themselves quite rudely and they hurt; others, however, step into our world and they bring sunshine and joy.

I have discovered that there are many serendipitous moments available to those who position themselves to receive them. Some of the grandest experiences of my life were couched in moments of darkness and uncertainty. Had I chosen the "Chicken Little" approach to life- "The sky is falling approach"—I would have succumbed to despair. Rather, I did not allow myself to panic and as a result a wonderful, unexpected back door blessing came my way.

I witness the same thing all the time in my ministry. I continue to marvel at the harsh realities that many people face in life. Though I am not in full-time pastoral ministry any longer, in my interim roles I routinely provide hospital ministry to families in crisis. It is not uncommon in those moments of trauma for remarkable and unusual things to occur. If I had only seen these phenomena once or twice in my ministry I would think nothing of it. But I have seen strange things happen in those moments time and again. In fact, they happen so routinely I almost expect them now.

Something serendipitous happens. Death lingers for a day or two until a long lost loved one comes home. Relationships that are strained or broken are mysteriously/miraculously mended just before death. Sometimes it comes in the form of an unexpected check or a phone call. But serendipity is there!

One of the marvelous things about God is his surprising nature. I chuckle at those who deem God to be wholly predictable. They box God in and defy him to step beyond those boundaries. Fundamentalism is particularly vulnerable to this accusation. Fundamentalist theology does not allow God any wiggle room. I would challenge that wrongheaded thinking for one thing is certain about God: while his character and attributes are steady and dependable, his actions can often surprise us. Actually, they ought to surprise us for God is God and thus can act and respond in any fashion he desires. Out of his dependable character, God then often surprises us with grace filled moments that are serendipitous.

Listen to the stories and testimonies that surround us. Most are filled with eureka moments where God sneaked into an event and surprised everyone. I love such stories for they speak of a grace of which we often sing but rarely encounter. Look around. Listen. Slow down. God is everywhere in his world working uniquely and mysteriously. Like Candid Camera, "when you least expect it," God shows up on the scene of life to bless and surprise. It is serendipitous and it is great fun.

The Death Bed

IT WAS ONE OF THE MOST INTERESTING and uplifting
bereavement calls I ever made while in pastoral ministry. I
know for some the terms "uplifting" and "bereavement" do
not belong in the same sentence but in this case it was true.
Often it is true when the death is that of one who had a
strong relationship with God.

The call came early one Saturday morning. A dear
saint of God had died in her sleep the night before.
Knowing the family well I did not have to change into my
"preacher duds" to enter their home. Dressed in casual
attire I arrived at the home just after the funeral home had
removed the body from its deathbed. I spoke with the
surviving son and his family and they asked me to lead
them in prayer. I did so and I remember thanking God for
the life and legacy of the dear lady that had just died.

We visited a moment and then the family asked that
I look at something in the bedroom where the body of the
dear lady was found. I am not squeamish or superstitious in

matters like this but I did find it rather odd that I be invited into that holy place of death. I soon found out why.

In the bedroom of the home was a beautiful antique oak bed. It was a classic piece with the distinctive honey oak hue that provided the rich beauty of the bed. The son sat on the edge of the bed still bearing the wrinkled and tangled sheets that only moments before had held the body of his dead mother. He started to reminisce with me about his mother and that old oak bed. He recalled the nights as a child when he had slept in that bed between his mother and father when lighting and thunder had scared him too much to sleep alone. He laughed about bouncing on the bed with his cousins. Truthfully, I had a lot to do that day and I did not plan to stay a long time but when he told me the full story of the bed I must admit that I was intrigued.

The bed was a family heirloom that was handcrafted by the deceased woman's father. No one really knew how old the bed really was but at the time of her death but we knew that it was at least eighty-six years old. How did we know? The lady was born in that same bed eighty-six years earlier. At that moment I felt such an unusual and spiritual sensation. The emotion swept over me like an ocean wave. This dear friend and saint of God had died in the same bed in which she was born.

I have never experienced that kind of cyclical significance in my life. Our society has so institutionalized the moment of death that it is rare indeed when a person even dies at home. Whereas it was once customary to take folks home to die, the opposite is true today. A recent survey indicated that 45% of the elderly in America are transferred to a hospital just prior to their death. That is a sad and cold statistic of our approach to death.

I was overwhelmed to look at that old oak bed and realize that this was both the birth bed and deathbed of a lovely lady. At that moment I realized that my thinking was in error. This was no deathbed. It always had been and always would be a birthing bed. For this dear lady even in death was birthed into her eternal home. Like Jacob of old she died with her feet in her own bed. What a blessing, what a change from the norm, and what a powerful symbol for those of us left behind: physically and spiritually birthed in the same bed. Thanks be to God for those holy reminders that come our way.

Frightening Trend in the Church

As MANY OF YOU KNOW BY NOW, I have this thing for the church. I love the church. I enjoy being with the people of God and I enjoy serving in any capacity that enhances and strengthens the Body of Christ. So it was no surprise to my friends that within weeks of my arrival in North Carolina I was back "at it again,"—serving as an interim pastor here in Shelby. I was blessed during my years in Tennessee to serve as the interim pastor of several wonderful congregations. I still maintain strong ties to those churches and I love and miss them all!

I enjoy my role in helping churches and helping pastors. Currently I am assisting a church that is in terrible need so that all of my experience both as a pastor and as an interim is serving me quite nicely.

Sadly this very strong and vibrant congregation recently endured what is commonly called a "split." After a less than stable two-year relationship between pastor and parish, the pastor and almost half the congregation left abruptly to join with another community of faith. The effect upon the church that I am now serving has been nothing short of devastating. There is a great deal of anger, betrayal, and mystery that shrouds the congregation. Many still don't know what happened to them. In fact the pastor's sudden departure has been described as having the same impact of a suicide. He left the church with no note of explanation.

Having trod this path before, I am now perceived to be a rather clairvoyant person in the community. Knowing none of the personalities involved, I have been able to fill in the gaps for the congregation in a way that mystifies many of them. "Who told you these things," they ask? "How did you know that our former pastor did thus and so?" "You must have talked to someone."

"It's simple," I said. "The vast majority of today's young ministers are rolling off the assembly line from theological cookie cutter factories once called seminaries. They are offered a vision of ministry now that is veiled in biblical doctrine but could be not be further from biblical truth." I then offered some generic themes that clearly struck a chord with the congregation. Those themes included, in part, the following: a dictatorial pastoral leadership style, an absence of servant ministry, a manipulative spirit that gathered key personalities into a closed society of "spiritually superior" persons, and a complete rejection of anything that smacks of traditional pastoral ministry.

Add to the list an unwillingness to visit members in the hospitals because they weren't "prospects," an unlisted number at the pastor's home, and the picture of the absence of a truly pastoral leader emerged in this very fine but deeply wounded congregation.

The sad thing is that what I am now mopping up and shoveling out of the corridors of this wounded church is happening at an alarming rate all over the country. These folks are fooled. They think I am a genius because I am interpreting in great detail what they have endured. I am no genius. I simply have sense enough to look around and to see a frightening and growing trend that is devastating the church.

And what scares me even further is that when my work is eventually done in this congregation, there will be scores of other congregations that will need the same help.

As my current role continues I am already planting seeds of hope and caution. The hope is that God will prosper his church and that the church will survive; the caution is for the committee that begins the task of selecting a new pastor. That committee must be driven by the biblical mandate to be as "wise as serpents and as harmless as doves." In this case, they will be as wise as serpents for they have seen in their former pastor the very essence of what that term means. And the image is as frightening as any creature that slithers under a rock!

Tommy

IN ALL OF MY YEARS OF MINISTRY, Tommy stands out as the most unique and challenging person I've ever dealt with. While serving a church in Kentucky during my seminary days, I came to know Tommy as both a delight and a nightmare. Tommy was an enormous, physically imposing man. He must have stood six-feet five inches tall and he easily weighed two hundred and fifty pounds. Tommy was a giant of man who happened to be mentally challenged.

When I arrived at the church I was quickly warned that Tommy was a problem. He liked to be involved in the life of the church but there were very few things he could do. In addition to his physical and emotional limitations, Tommy had a serious problem with personal hygiene. To be perfectly blunt, Tommy reeked of body odor and his clothing was normally dirty and wrinkled. To the credit of the church most overlooked Tommy's hygiene problems while always searching for answers as to how to address a delicate and smelly problem.

One Christmas the ladies of the church stumbled onto what we all believed was a brilliant and failsafe plan to assist Tommy with his problem. They decided to put together a Christmas basket for Tommy. The idea was truly well intentioned and came with the love and concern of the church. There were candies, fruit, socks, gloves, and other small gifts. The men of the church contributed to a cash gift which was also in the basket. Here is where it got interesting: the "brilliant" idea of the ladies was to also include wash clothes, soap, shampoo, and deodorant. Their thinking was that Tommy would use the gifts given to them and subsequently improve his condition (and the odors in the church). These ladies could not have been more wrong!

I chuckle when I recall the night the church gave Tommy his gift. Like a child this simple man tore into his Christmas basket. He sorted through all of the gifts, shoved the candy in his mouth, and the cash into his pockets. It was then that the brilliant idea unraveled before our very eyes. With great care Tommy began to pick out the items of personal hygiene that had been the genesis of the basket to start with, and he sat those items aside. A small pile of soap, shampoo, and wash clothes were pulled from the basket, leaving only the candy, fruit, and socks. With a mouthful of gum and candy, Tommy boldly declared that he had no use for those other things. Those "other" things were the very items Tommy needed the most.

We left the church that night knowing that Tommy would be back the following Sunday smelling and looking the same as always. We had tried to help him but, in truth, he did not know how to receive the assistance we offered. I don't know if anyone else in the church learned a lesson that night but I certainly did.

I realized that I am no different than Tommy when it comes to the grace gifts of God. There have been countless times in my journey when God has blessed me with baskets of goodies. Those baskets are filled with an assortment of gifts. Some are for my pleasure and some are for my good. Often, like poor Tommy, I too have sorted through God's gifts to me and taken only the things that I wanted, not the things that I needed.

Our attempt to assist Tommy backfired that night but it served as a stark and graphic reminder to a young minister about the manner in which we often receive the gifts of God. All of his gifts are for our benefit. Some we want; some we don't. But they are all given for our enjoyment and blessing. May God help us all to accept the gifts that come our way, and may he include with them a portion of wisdom to know how to unwrap them all.

10 Annoyances in the Church

I TEND TO BE A LIST PERSON. Most every day I will jot down a list of things I need to do so that I don't forget. Sometimes I take notes of sermons I want to preach, research I need to pursue, or the grocery items I need to pick up. With that said I have been compiling a list for some time of the things that annoy me the most in church. I have developed the "top ten things that aggravate me in church." The list is mine and mine alone; perhaps you agree or disagree but these things drive me crazy in the house of God. Unlike Letterman, in no particular order, I offer my top ten list:

1. Cell phones or beepers that go off in the middle of church. Turn the things off when you are in God's house or if it is absolutely necessary put it on silent mode; you are there not to hear an earthly word but a "thus says the Lord" word. Plus your neighbor doesn't need to be interrupted in worship.

2. Parents that try to silence noisy children and in the process make more noise than the child ever did. Children will make noise and create a stir in church. That much is given. Moms and dads who "shush" their children loudly often are more distracting than the child.

3. Music ministers who read the words to the hymn the congregation is about to sing. Often they say things like, "listen to the powerful words of this hymn." Well, the congregation is about to sing the words of that hymn; get out of their way and let them sing the words themselves. If the song is that strong it doesn't need anyone to promote its message. If it is good it will carry itself.

4. Soloists who "attempt" to sing with canned music and the machine doesn't work. So they stand there tapping their feet and twiddling their thumbs waiting for someone to fix it. And then when the music does start I am amazed at all of the nearsighted singers who don't know the words to the song and attempt to read them from the back of a cassette cover and can't see the tiny print. So they botch the song and make fools of themselves.

5. Candy and cough drop wrappers. Some folk must have hidden microphones in their hands for when they unwrap a mint the sound is amplified all over the church. If you must unwrap a piece of candy, at least be discreet about it.

6. Snoring. What can you say? Sadly, in many churches there is great reason to snore. But it is an offensive sound in the house of God. I have heard chainsaws that were quieter than some snores. Try breath-right or something but leave that noise outside or on the pillow.

7. The clicking noise of fingernail clippers. This one is a mystery to me. Why on earth do some folks trim their nails in God's house? Every church has a nail clipping fool. Not only is the sound disruptive but also it is a nasty habit. No one wants to clean up someone else's fingernails. Leave it at home

8. Overly indulged perfume odors. I have an allergic reaction to the smell of perfume or cologne. It affects my throat; I start coughing and my bronchia tightens. Some people smell as if they have bathed in the stuff. Take my word for it—"a little dab will do ya!" And it will do for others, too.

9. Ill prepared preachers. If the preaching event is as sacred as we proclaim it to be then why don't more preachers put time into preparing their sermons? A wing and a prayer are offensive to God. And one more thing. Preachers, try reading your scripture before Sunday morning. Stumbling over words and names is a clear indication to your congregation that you haven't worked the text very carefully.

10. The bathroom parade. I have been to churches where at some point in the service it feels like the entire congregation makes a dash to the bathroom door. Certainly there are times that folks must leave the sanctuary. But taking a number for the bathroom door is inexcusable. Often it is the same offenders week after week and it needs to stop.

There you have it. My top ten list of things that annoy me in church. Believe it or not even as I complete my top ten grievances, another list is developing. There will be more on that later.

Upside Down Kingdom

I THINK I FINALLY HAVE STARTED TO understand some of the basic premises of the Kingdom of God and one of the lessons I learned came from a highly unusual source. While watching a rerun of the Seinfeld show, I caught a glimpse of the Kingdom through the hapless character known as George Costanza. George is a classic loser! There is no other way to describe him. George testifies to his own inadequacies and ineptness in an episode in which he decides that he will live his life by doing the opposite of what he normally does. Determining that his life is already wasted by the decisions he has made (that were all wrong), George figures that it can't hurt to try another approach and so he reasons that if his instincts are always wrong, he must do the opposite. The culmination of this logic comes when he meets a lovely young lady. Whereas the "old" George would try to impress her with tall tales of being a successful architect or a marine biologist, the opposite George strolls up to her and says, "My name is George. I am single, unemployed, and I live with my parents." Amazingly, the opposite response won the heart of the young lady.

In a recent study of the Sermon on the Mount, I found myself struggling with the implications of the message of Jesus. Everything he taught in those chapters runs contrary to the human instincts and responses we all possess. The theological key, for me, came from the unlikely character of George Costanza that the opposite is required. Once you unlock that thought, it is easy to understand the Sermon.

The Sermon on the Mount is Jesus' way of introducing us to the Kingdom he sought to establish by showing us the unique ways we are to live. The standard that he set in the Sermon is a standard that no mere human can live by. The things he asks us to do are impossible at best and ludicrous at worst! How can we, for example, "turn the other cheek and go the extra mile." None of us in our own power and strength are fueled for that kind of response. We are more attuned to punching the nose and dropping the bag but that is not the response that the Kingdom demands.

So how do we live like the Kingdom? We have to recognize that the Kingdom of God is an upside down

Kingdom. It is contrary to the ways of this world. It is the opposite of what we humanly believe it ought to be. That is where a George Costanza "theology" can help us. Look at life in this world through Kingdom lenses and it will turn the values and the standards of this culture on its ear. With Kingdom lens everything is the opposite and everything is upside down.

Thus the stakes are higher for than ever before. American Christians are especially susceptible to blending into the surrounding and looking like the culture. Often we are not the opposite of our culture as representatives of God's Kingdom but we are the very epitome of that culture. The distinctiveness that is demanded of us is lost from the pressures around us.

Listen to Costanza but live like Christ. Try the opposite. It won't look like anything you've ever done before. But it is not supposed to, is it?

Why They Don't Come

WE WONDER WHY FOLKS DON'T want to attend church? I recently visited with a young minister who was wounded and bleeding from a recent event in his church. He had just returned from vacation re-energized and revitalized for ministry. The time away was good for his spirits and body. He also needed it for the hectic schedule that awaited him and his congregation.

As he entered the church building upon his return he should have sensed that something was wrong. Rather than welcoming their pastor back from vacation several church members turned their heads and walked away without saying a word. He didn't think anything about it at the time other than the response was out of character. He would soon learn why.

After the service a group of church leaders asked to visit with him. They quickly informed the minister that there had been a called secret meeting of the church's leadership while he was on vacation and they had decided that he was no longer welcome there. He was stunned. A secret meeting? Didn't the constitution and by-laws strictly forbid such gatherings without prior notice to the church? What had he done or not done? Who knew about this meeting? Who was there? Did the church vote on this? A plethora of questions spewed forth from the confused young man. There were lots of questions and very few answers that were forthcoming.

He was handed a script of his resignation letter. If he read it the following Sunday there would be a modicum of severance pay to be offered; if he refused to read the script, he would receive nothing. In the church some call that grace. In the secular world it is outright blackmail and it is an affront to everything that is good and decent in God's world.

After the initial shock wore off and he found his footing the young minister asked why no one had spoken to him about potential problems. Why wasn't he warned and asked to correct behaviors? If he had known perhaps he could have changed some things.

The answer was as pitiful as anything I've ever heard. The only church leader that had the guts to speak lowered his head and mumbled, "Well, preacher, we tried to give you hints and drop clues but you didn't pick up on 'em."

I was speechless. I asked the young man, "You mean they actually said that?" "Yes, sir was the reply." They dropped hints. When did hints equate with forthrightness and truthfulness? To manipulate the constitutional documents of the church is one thing but to trample on the truth is another.

When will we get it? When will the church stop playing games with the truth, with each other, and God? When will we stop being so cruel and malicious in our behavior? When will we quit behaving like the world and start mirroring the spirit of Christ?

I continue to marvel that the church remains as viable as it does. In some cases it ought not. When secret meetings and vindictive behavior rule the day, the church does not stand a chance. We must reinvent ourselves. We must rediscover the gospel of God—a gospel of grace, redemption, forgiveness, the extra mile, and good old fashioned, honest-to-goodness love. Until we do there is no question why folks don't attend our churches.

You can't blame them. I wouldn't either!

Worship Connection

WHY EXACTLY DO WE WORSHIP? Or does the question need to be reframed? Maybe the question today is not about "why" but about "whom?"

While scrolling through the television this past Sunday in the early hours of dawn, I stumbled upon one television worship service after another. Some commanded my attention and I paused for a moment. Others were less appealing and were very much appalling so I kept the remote in my hand for a quick exit. One in particular caught my eye and my ear. One particularly cool preacher had a very catchy commercial. He is one of those hip preachers who use props on the stage. It is not unusual to see him in blue jeans and a tee shirt, sitting in a boat or behind the wheel of a convertible that have been positioned on stage. He has beads around his neck, his hair is semi-spiked and he is cool. I don't care if he is cool or really how he dresses. But I do care what he has to say? What "god" does he promote? That is my question. So I lingered on the channel for the moment and my question was quickly answered.

The commercial for this "preacher" is really slick and it is seductive in all of the wrong ways. There must be twenty people who have been prompted to speak to the camera and say, "I connected with (the preacher's name)." The point is clear. These persons made a connection of some sort with the hip "preacher." I felt like I was watching a fan club commercial. This guy is cool, this guy is hip. I connect with this guy.

But is that what constitutes worship? I listened very carefully to these infomercials and God was never, ever mentioned. Not once! Relationships were high on the list. So was connection. All of the glib post-modern clichés and hooks were present. But God was conspicuously absent from the production. And it caused me to wonder, "Whatever happened to God?"

A nearby church in my community has a slogan that is plastered all over our town. The church is not playing by traditional rules and has a target for innovative audiences. The slogan for the church reads, "Where People Are Our Passion." I think I understand their sentiment in attempting to reach a diverse population and I commend them for that. But whatever happened to God?

I had lunch with a pastor recently. He was telling me about the good things happening in his church and from all indicators the church is doing well. We talked about worship for a while and something in his remarks prompted me to ask him the question, "How do you define worship?" His answer was stunning and I quote: "Worship is where we gather to connect with each other." I sat silent for a moment and I asked one more question. "Steve," I asked, "isn't there Someone missing from your equation?" He muffled a laugh and said, "Oh, yeah, God." But had I not inserted God into the conversation, God would have been left out just as He was left out of my friends understanding of worship. Whatever happened to God?

Increasingly in our image savvy culture God is being squeezed out of the equation as too old fashioned, too traditional, and too politically incorrect. Well, call me a fuddy-duddy but if God is not in that which the church promotes, the church is no longer the church. I can stay home on Sunday and read the paper if worship is about "connecting" with a razzle dazzle showman, or "connecting" with people. I connect with lots of people all week long. If that is all worship promotes, I don't need it.

But I do need God. I hunger for God. I thirst for God. I need to worship God. And it saddens me that the church of all people seems to have forgotten about the One who called us into existence.

The question still lingers, doesn't it? Whatever happened to God?

The Author

Danny M. West is a native of Gloucester, Virginia. A graduate of Carson-Newman College in Jefferson City, Tennessee, he holds the M.Div., Th.M., and Ph.D. degrees from the Southern Baptist Theological Seminary in Louisville, Kentucky. Dr. West has served as the pastor of churches in Indiana, Kentucky, and Tennessee. He is currently serving in the capacity of interim pastor for his tenth congregation.

Dr. West is an Associate Professor of Preaching in the School of Divinity at Gardner-Webb University in Boiling Springs, North Carolina. Additionally, he directs the Doctor of Ministry program, oversees ministerial referral services, and provides administrative support to the school.

He is widely published in the area of preaching books and journals. He has contributed to: *A Cloud of Witnesses: Sermon Illustrations from the Christian Heritage; From Our Christian Heritage: Hundreds of Ways to Add*

Christian History in Teaching, Preaching, and Writing; The Pulpit Digest; Proclaim Magazine; The Minister's Manual; Preaching Magazine; John Killinger: Celebrating 75 Years, and many other religious and institutional journals. In addition, he has reviewed a number of books on preaching for *The Review and Expositor.* His doctoral dissertation was entitled "The Preaching Ministry of Theodore F. Adams."

Dr. West and his wife, Jeanne, reside in Shelby, North Carolina.

www.ingramcontent.com/pod-product-compliance
Lightning Source LLC
Chambersburg PA
CBHW021335090426
42742CB00008B/618